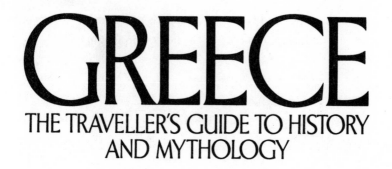

GREECE

THE TRAVELLER'S GUIDE TO HISTORY AND MYTHOLOGY

BRIAN DICKS

DAVID & CHARLES
Newton Abbot   London   North Pomfret (Vt)

For Alcibiades and his relations and friends –
Mario, Dimitris, Yota, Harry and Irini

By the same author

The Ancient Persians: How They Lived and Worked
Corfu
The Greeks: How They Live and Work
The Israelis: How They Live and Work
The Isle of Wight
Rhodes

British Library Cataloguing in Publication Data

Dicks, Brian
  Greece.
  1. Greece – History
  I. Title
  949.5   DF757

  ISBN 0–7153–7797–3

Typeset by
Northern Phototypesetting Co., Bolton
and printed in Great Britain
by Redwood Burn Limited, Trowbridge & Esher
for David & Charles (Publishers) Limited
Brunel House, Newton Abbot, Devon

Published in the United States of America
by David & Charles Inc.
North Pomfret, Vermont 05053 USA

Contents

The author wishes to thank Mr Lothar Wuttke for the line illustrations in this book. The photographs marked with an asterisk at the end of the captions are by the author. The others are reproduced by permission of the National Tourist Organisation of Greece to whom the author and publishers are grateful.

Greece: political boundaries, regions and main centres

1

Concept and Environment

This book was written with travellers in mind, both those determined to sample a unique experience and see Greece for themselves, and those content to make the journey from the comfort of an armchair thus conjuring up their own highly personal images of a land of scenic contrasts, one rich in historical associations and animated by an exuberant, colourful and basically hospitable people. Yet though conceived for the traveller, the pages that follow are not a tourist guide in the conventional sense for the intention was never to provide a sequence of geographical itineraries or a series of detailed descriptions of panoramic views, natural curiosities and historical sites. Rather, this book is an attempt to paint, albeit with a bold and broad brush, the major episodes which have gone into the making of contemporary Greece and, hence, into the cultural characteristics of its people. The treatment, therefore, is chronological rather than topographical and though this makes it difficult to characterise individual regions, towns and settlements, it is hoped that the broad discourse on the country's ancient, medieval and modern development, and on many of its historical and contemporary figures, will serve to illustrate Greece's historical complexity, geographical diversity, and also its modern character and problems.

THE CONCEPT OF GREECE

'What is, or is not Greece,' stated Murray's *Encyclopaedia of Geography* (1834), 'is a question of no little difficulty . . . for the name was always applied under gradations.' Like all writers on the topic he was confronted with the intractable problem of definition, for in history 'Greece' was never an independent nation, self-contained within specific natural boundaries. Traditionally the term implied the southernmost tip of the Balkan peninsula and the islands surrounding it, but rarely did it refer to a fixed geographical area. Today, Murray's question may be answered in a banal fashion: Greece is a southern Balkan country of 132,562 square kilometres of mainland and islands projecting into the eastern Mediterranean and having political boundaries with Albania, Yugoslavia, Bulgaria and Turkey. Yet this territory is the creation of the nineteenth and twentieth centuries and in no way corresponds to the concept of the ancient Hellenic world, nor does it include all the regions inhabited by Greek speakers.

The date of Murray's publication coincided with the establishment of the modern independent nation which was wrested from the declining Ottoman empire after nearly 400 years of rule by the sultans of Constantinople. The Ottoman empire itself was the conqueror-inheritor of the fragmented Byzantine state of which the Greek mainland and islands were a part. Under Byzantium, Greece came nearest to nationhood, but even then the capital was Constantinople and the Greek homeland a mere province. The Fourth Crusade (1204) detached it from Byzantium and subdivided the mainland and islands into feudal counties and baronies which became pawns in the political and ideological game between the Catholic states of Western Europe, Byzantium and the expanding Moslem powers. In classical, Hellenistic and Roman times it is equally difficult to speak in any formal sense of a political geography, for Greece (or Hellas as the term was understood) was either a series of independent entities or a collection of provinces subject to more powerful empires. Common cultural grounds naturally existed, but variations in dialects and political structures produced distinct regionalisation. Collectively, however, the Hellenic world was sharply separated from the 'barbarian' provinces to the north, which meant that Greek civilisation and culture covered only part of the country as it is territorially and politically defined today. Conversely, it had important outliers in Cyprus and Egypt, along the Adriatic coast and throughout the western Mediterranean, particularly in southern Italy and Sicily. It further spanned the Euro-Asian boundary taking in the coasts of the Black Sea and western Anatolia. This latter area, mainly from the early medieval period onwards, formed the commercial and intellectual centre of gravity of the Greek world and played a fundamental role in the evolution of the modern state.

Though most historians and geographers would agree that human history is not simply a mechanical response to geographical factors, nevertheless, many of the characteristics of modern Greece are the fruits of immutable geographical constraints affecting social, economic and even intellectual attitudes today in much the same way they did 4,000 years ago. Murray's Greece in 1834 was an embryonic country, small in terms of population and in territorial extent. Yet it coincided in a remarkable way with the traditional concept of Greece as that area occupying the southern Mediterranean portion of the Balkans. Nineteenth- and twentieth-century boundary extensions, which were chiefly northwards, introduced a completely new set of geographical values, transforming the country into what has been described as both a Mediterranean and a Macedonian State. It acquired a territory which more than doubled its earlier size and the story of modern Greece can be interpreted as an attempt by a Mediterranean-orientated society to control, through settled frontiers, part of the Balkan interior. In the past, however, this had worked in the reverse direction with strongly based continental powers expanding their territorial influence southwards into the Greek peninsula and into the heart of the Aegean.

MOUNTAINS AND THE SEA

It has often been said that Greece is 'a land of the mountains and the sea'. Great areas of the country are over 900 m and many summits reach 1,800m. The highest mountain, Olympus, the traditional home of the gods, rises to 2,911m. The mountains stretch out as peninsulas which, in many cases, are continued into the Aegean as chains of islands. Gulfs and bays penetrate far inland, and few places in Greece are more than eighty kilometres from the coast. The coastal plain is usually narrow, but there are also numerous upland plains in the interior which have formed regions of settlement from earliest times.

In geological terms, Greece consists of blocks of old and resistant rocks occupying the north-eastern part of the country and the central Aegean islands, and a series of weaker and younger rocks, greatly folded during the Tertiary earth movements, occupying western and southern Greece. Subsequent fracturing and uplift has affected both zones and this instability has continued to the present time as the incidence of earthquakes indicates. The Aegean basin itself owes its very existence to recent faulting, as do the gulfs of Corinth and Patras which separate the Peloponnesus from the northern mainland. The presence of hot springs and a line of volcanic peaks stretching from the dormant cone of Methana in the Saronic Gulf, through Milos and Thera to Kos, provide further evidence of crustal weaknesses. The Kaimeni islands, rising in the centre of the explosive crater of Thera, are the new cones of a still active volcano. The most destructive earthquakes which have occurred during recent years took place in the Ionian islands of Cefalonia, Zante and Ithaca in 1953, in the Magnesia district of Thessaly in 1955 and in the island of Thera in 1956.

The most important natural feature of the country is a series of high mountain ranges (the Pindus) which extends southwards from Albania and Yugoslavia as an extension of the Dinaric Alps. This mountainous backbone of the Greek mainland is composed predominantly of limestone which gives rise to extensive areas of *karst* (eroded limestone) scenery with innumerable sink-holes, underground streams and bare waterless localities. The rugged inhospitable landscape has been intensified by recent faulting which has produced steep slopes, escarpments and deep ravines. The Pindus, therefore, provides a most effective barrier to communications between east and west, and astride it the country's main geographical and historical regions have evolved.

To the west of the main Pindus ranges, in Epirus and Acarnania, a series of longitudinal valleys and ranges lies parallel to the coast making east–west access difficult. To the east a number of mountainous appendages of the main range extend in a south-westerly direction, giving rise to rugged promontories which are continued into the Aegean as island chains. The large and elongated island of Euboea, together with Andros, Tinos and Myconos, is a structural continuation of the highlands of central Greece. The Cycladic islands are the exposed summits of the prolongation of the highlands of Boeotia and Attica and demonstrate the structural links between the Greek mainland and Asia Minor. To the south of the gulfs of Corinth and Patras the Pindus is continued as the wild and rugged limestone highlands of the Peloponnesus. From the central mountainous core of Arcadia the main chain can be traced southwards to the island of Cythera and then through Crete, Carpathos and Rhodes into Asia Minor. Structurally, Crete forms the southern mountainous rim of the Aegean basin.

The lowland element in the Greek landscape is not very considerable, but it has naturally played a very important role in the life of the country. Most of the coastal plains and interior basins were formed during the faulting of late Tertiary times, and in southern and western Greece they tend to be discontinuous and isolated features. The major areas of lowland are found in the north and east, of which the Plain of Thessaly is by far the most extensive and quite exceptional. In Macedonia and Thrace, river basins and alluvial lowlands are extensive, and separated by mountainous blocks of a complex geological history. Today Macedonia and Thessaly are the country's most advanced agricultural regions for their extensive lowlands have aided scientific farming and mechanisation.

CLIMATE AND VEGETATION

Greece is generally regarded as a Mediterranean country, but its climate is of a transitional character, with features of the continental climate of eastern Europe as well as the distinguishing marks of the Mediterranean regime. The distribution of mountains and lowlands and the indented nature of the coastline emphasise strongly the effect of location on climate. On the one hand the mountainous character of much of the country carries continental conditions as far south as the central Peloponnesus; on the other hand the numerous bays and gulfs allow the influences of the Mediterranean Sea to penetrate in places far into the highlands. The result of both these controls is seen in the great variety of local climates. In general terms, however, the interior of northern and central Greece, and to a lesser extent the Peloponnesian highlands, can be said to experience a continental climate where snow is common in winter, and the remainder of the country, southern Greece and the islands, share the Mediterranean characteristics. Warm, wet winters and hot, dry summers, with frequent blue skies and rainfall that is concentrated in the form of heavy showers during the winter months, is the textbook definition of the Mediterranean regime. For the reasons already given, however, there are considerable local variations of this pattern, particularly in rainfall totals.

Greece's natural vegetation is obviously related to the variable patterns of its climatological regimes where both altitude and latitude govern the characteristic species, though today this pattern has been greatly altered because of the activities of man over the centuries. A typical Mediterranean vegetation occurs in southern Greece where trees, shrubs and small plants are adapted to withstand the summer drought. Oak, laurel, oleander and juniper are common species, together with conifers such as the cypress and Aleppo pine. Many of the smaller species have a winter and spring growing season and a summer resting period. Spring is a strikingly colourful season, where by the end of April cyclamens, anemones, poppies, mimosa, wistaria and a host of fruit trees blossom in profusion. The contrast between spring and summer is most striking in Attica and the Aegean islands, the latter season producing a sun-parched landscape. In the highlands of southern Greece and at lower altitudes in the north the character of the vegetation changes as summer rainfall and winter cold increase. Deciduous oak, chestnut and beech on the lower and middle slopes grade into conifers at higher altitudes, and above the tree line alpine pastures or rock flora predominate.

LANDSCAPE CHANGES

The broad lineaments of Greek geography have changed little over the centuries, but there is now strong evidence to suggest that its early peopling, and the subsequent establishment of regional cultures in ancient times, took place against an environmental background that, in terms of vegetation cover at least, was substantially different from what it is today. Meagre yet suggestive evidence for the more prolific growth of forest communities in the past is derived from archaeology and pollen analysis and this is strongly supported by the comments and references of the ancient and classical writers. Though climatic changes might well have had some effect on the reduction of the country's original vegetation cover, it is now accepted that the impact of human activity, in the form of centuries of burning for clearing, over-grazing and general mismanagement, was chiefly responsible for its progressive destruction. The direct result of over-exploitation has led to the secondary growth of a dense tangle of thorny undergrowth known as *maquis*, which is a mixed plant community of largely aromatic bushes, where one species rarely dominates. A further stage of degeneration is reached in the *garigue*, a term applied to stony dried-out ground with small scattered bushes, many of them again aromatic – sage, rosemary, lavender, thyme, rue and garlic.

Tantalising though Plato's works are to modern interpretation, he provides many graphic sketches of the Greek environment, comparing the countryside of his day with what it had been, or he thought it had been, in the past. In the *Critias* he talks of abundant woodlands of which only traces existed: 'For although some of the mountains now only afford sustenance to bees, not so long ago there were still to be seen roofs of timber cut from the trees growing there, which were of a size sufficient to cover the largest houses.' In the Homeric writings ancient woodlands and groves figured largely in religious beliefs and ceremonies, and there are numerous examples of consecrated woodlands that came under rigorous protection. The Homeric *Hymn to Aphrodite* talks of the nymphs and groves of Mount Idha whose trees 'no mortal fells with iron'. This and similar references might well suggest, of course, that even in ancient times, woodlands were not all that common and needed conservation. Many of Homer's similes, however, are of great interest in providing plant and tree associations: in the *Iliad* Sarpendon 'falls as an oak, or a silver poplar, or a slim pine tree', and another hero is brought down 'like an ash that on the crest of a far-seen hill is smitten with the axe of bronze, and brings the delicate foliage to the ground'.

Homer's reference to the axe singles out one of the three traditional enemies of the Mediterranean vegetation cover, the other two being fire and the goat. These processes of irrational cutting, clearing and over-grazing have continued to the present day and have been intensified by periods of invasion, wars and foreign domination. Early Greek agriculture was, of necessity, a shifting type which meant the progressive clearance of virgin land, and there is little evidence that fertilisation was practised, so that constant encroachments on woodlands were necessary. Timber for domestic building, for shipbuilding and for charcoal manufacturing for the production of metal tools, weapons and ornaments, also took its toll on the natural vegetation. Homer constantly refers to the work of the woodcutters, but perhaps the most evocative simile is that of the 'mules that throw their great strength into the draught, and drag out of the mountain down a rugged track some beam or huge ship-timber, and their hearts are spent in toil and sweat'. The life of most classical city states depended on their navies and hence timber-producing regions were of upmost importance. According to Herodotus, Histiaeus built a fortress on the Thracian coast where 'ship-building timber is boundless' and when Athens lost the city of Amphipolis in 424BC the loss of an important timber supply was of graver consequence than the loss of general commercial revenue.

Woodlands were also the home of herds of swine and

provided sustenance for other livestock, particularly goats. Such grazing greatly hindered regeneration and even man, it seems, contributed to this process, for Herodotus refers to the 'acorn-eating' Arcadians. Apart from the deliberate abuse, there was the forest fire which during the dry Greek summer (as now) caused serious damage. Another of Homer's descriptions compares the devastation of a particular area to a fire that 'rages through the valleys of a summer-dried mountain, and the deep forest burns'. Whether natural or man-induced, fires were commonplace and highly destructive.

The ancient writers were well aware of the consequences of woodland abuse and of the function of trees in assuring the perennial flow of springs and thereby contributing one of the elements of soil fertility. Forest clearance led to the upset of the micro-climate near the surface of the soil with the result that the humus content decreased and the fertility of the soil declined rapidly leading to deterioration and erosion. It has been suggested that by the beginning of classical times the hillsides of Mediterranean Greece were scoured by erosion and the rivers were choked with silt. 'No more in the dells', cries Theocritis, 'no more in the groves, no more in the woodlands. Farewell, Arethusa! Farewell the rivers!'

The destructive exploitation of the Greek landscape continued into the Middle Ages, and beyond, with timber being constantly sought for ships, houses, mineral smelting and all domestic requirements. Shipbuilding in particular took considerable toll of the Greek forests for the Romans, Byzantines, Venetians and Turks were all maritime peoples, and little appears to have been done to reafforest. Moreover, the process of natural seeding was checked continually by the voracity of the goat to whose undiscriminating palate new shoots and young seedlings proved irresistible. A great increase in sheep and goat rearing is attributable to the Slavs who settled throughout Greece in the Middle Ages (see Chapter 4).

2

The Wine~Dark Sea

The earliest beginnings of Greece still flounder in the mists of mythology, but this is a country where the step from fable into the light of history is often a short and a quick one. Since the end of the nineteenth century many remarkable archaeological discoveries, coupled with developments in the reinterpretation of Greek legend and saga, have given a certain, though still very basic, historical respectability to the stories and traditions which earlier scholars had rejected outright as inventive fancy.

The classical Greeks treated their traditions quite differently as historical records, of a certain kind, to be criticised and used in the appropriate way. Thucydides, discussing Greece's earliest events in the first book of his *Peloponnesian War*, believed he was dealing with historical material, because the great epic poems of Homer, the *Iliad* and the *Odyssey*, contained credible historical figures whose actions often took place in precise geographical settings. Yet it was the complex intermixture of credibility with supernatural happenings and obvious mythological personalities which, in 1846, caused George Grote to write in his monumental *History of Greece:* 'The times which I thus set apart from the regions of history are discernible only through a different atmosphere – that of epic poetry and legend. To confound together these disparate matters is, in my judgment, essentially unphilosophical.' Thus historians generally accepted that the history of Greece began with the first recorded Olympiad in 776BC; everything prior to that date was assumed to be legend invented by the Greeks, with their inexhaustible ability for improvisation, to fill in the chronological blanks of their uncertain past.

Then in 1876 came one of the greatest moments in archaeology when the German amateur excavator, Heinrich

Minoan and Mycenaean sites in the Southern Aegean

Schliemann, uncovered the royal shaft graves at Mycenae and telegraphed King George I of the Hellenes, 'I have gazed upon the face of Agamemnon.' In actual fact the beaten gold 'mask of Agamemnon' was several centuries earlier than the time of the Homeric king, but the real significance of Schliemann's discoveries was their unequivocal support of the general reliability of tradition and folk memory. At Mycenae, as at Troy, he brought to light cities uncommonly like those described by Homer, and subsequently, Sir Arthur Evans, equally motivated to prove the truth in tradition, excavated the palace complex of King Minos at Knossos in Crete and other sites in his island empire. In more recent times legend after legend has been substantiated – in some cases to an astonishing degree – by modern archaeological discoveries, forcing a continual reappraisal of early Greek history. Questions of fact, or palpable fiction, or a compromise between these extremes continue to guide the attitudes and researches of scholars, but if the past has set the precedent then new discoveries will only confirm the basic accuracy of the Greek myths.

PELASGIANS AND IONIANS

In a cultural-linguistic sense the earliest known peoples of the Greek mainland, the islands and the Aegean coasts of Asia Minor were not Greek at all for they spoke a language which the ancients would have termed 'barbarian', that is, non-Hellenic. Thucydides and Herodotus refer to them as Pelasgians – which probably meant aborigines – and some survived until classical times speaking a language unintelligible to them. The Pelasgians belonged to the dark-haired 'Mediterranean' race and are now thought of as part of a greater series of migrations which brought them from Asia Minor and/or North Africa after 2500BC. Cave sites and rock shelters were their most common habitations, but the occurrence of some fortified settlements introduces for the first time a recurring feature in the prehistory and history of Greece – the possibility of conquest and government by relatively small bands of well-organised invaders.

It seems safe to regard the word Pelasgian as one used by Greek speakers for the people they found in possession when they first moved into the peninsula (around 2000BC) from the north. The process of this Greek infiltration and conquest might well be symbolically illustrated in one of the best known of Athenian folk tales which tells of a contest between the local goddess Athena and the god Poseidon for possession of the Acropolis. As a bribe rather than as a weapon of war, Poseidon produced the horse, but Athena offered the olive-tree, which for the Attic environment was judged the more useful gift. So Athens was called after her and Athena, as goddess of war, the patron of arts and crafts and the personification of wisdom, was worshipped on the Acropolis. Poseidon, who appears to be a Greek or, more strictly speaking, an Hellenic god, also obtained recognition in Athens and became particularly famous as father of the city's national hero Theseus. This contest, often retold in classical times, is featured on the west pediment of the Parthenon, though now only two mutilated figures remain. The central motif was accidentally destroyed in 1687 and the rest, badly damaged, was taken to London in 1803. An accurate reproduction of the pediment, however, is housed in the museum on the Acropolis.

It is tempting to read into this story of Athena and Poseidon the folk memory of a clash in Attica of migrant Greek speakers with the indigenous inhabitants, a collision which found a peaceful issue with the natives absorbing the incomers. The Athenians were one of two groups in southern Greece who claimed to be autochthonous or 'born of the soil'; the Arcadians were the other who settled in the wild and mountainous terrain of the central Peloponnesus when their Pelasgian neighbours at Argos battled with the Greeks. These remnants, suggestive of earlier peoples in both areas, can be explained on geographical grounds. Arcadia, as the Turks found later, is traditionally difficult to conquer and its comparative security was subsequently idealised in its image as the home of pastoral poetry and song, and a land inhabited by shepherds, nymphs, satyrs and other mythological characters. As for Attica, the territory of the Athenians, its thin unproductive soils, which Plato was to describe as 'the bones of a body wasted with disease' might well have proved unattractive to these earliest Greeks. That they were an inland people unfamiliar with Mediterranean conditions is illustrated by the fact that they had no words in their Greek language for such natural and cultivated species as the olive, fig, cypress, vine, narcissus, bean and hyacinth. Most significantly, the very name for sea – *thalassa* – with which Greece is traditionally associated, is not Greek – further proof, it seems, of their continental origin.

Place names for towns, rivers and other natural features are of further help in charting the progress and characteristics of the earliest inhabitants of Greece. Those with the common endings –*nthos* (Corinthos), –*ttos* (Hymettos) and –*ssos* (Ilissos, Tylissos, Halicarnassos) are not Greek in origin, and in Crete, in particular, there are scores of such old place names of which Knossos itself is the most obvious example. Neither is –*enai* a Greek suffix and this is of special interest to the above argument because Athens (Athenai in Greek) and its patron goddess are names which predate the arrival of the first Greek speakers. Of all the ancient Greek cities, the 'royal' houses of Athens and

Argos have the longest genealogies, dating back to 1700BC, and it is of further interest that both were conspicuous among Greek cities in having a goddess as their chief patron in the face of predominantly male Hellenic deities. This possibly reflected an entirely different concept of religion and many scholars have regarded the god-concept as central European and the goddess-concept as Mediterranean, Athena and the Argive Hera being derived in straight descent from the nature goddess and other cults of Crete. Certainly Crete was initially occupied by non-Greek speakers and the island was destined to play a major and formative role in the prehistory of the Aegean and the southern Greek mainland.

CRETE AND THE MINOANS

The long narrow island of Crete, 260 kilometres from east to west and varying in width from 12 to 60 kilometres, is the largest of all Greek islands and the fourth in size in the Mediterranean. Known to the Greeks as the 'sixth continent', Crete is the physical extension of a great mountainous arc which, via Cythera, Crete itself, Carpathos and Rhodes, structurally links the Peloponnesus and the Greek mainland with the ranges of western Anatolia. The backbone of the island is a series of high mountainous blocks extending from the Lefki Ori or White Mountains in the west, reaching 8,045ft (2,452m), through the Idha range or Psiloritis (8,058ft; 2,456m) in the centre, to the Dhikti Mountains (7,047ft; 2,148m) and Sitia Mountains (4,843ft; 1,476m) in the east. Thus both structurally and topographically Crete can be regarded as a great bastion shutting off the Greek Aegean from the Egyptian and Libyan sections of the eastern Mediterranean, and the fact, too, that the island's main harbours are confined to its irregular northern coast has intensified this Aegean orientation.

Yet wider geographical values were responsible for Crete's precocious development in prehistory. Situated almost equidistant between the Greek mainland, Asia Minor and North Africa the island, by virtue of this position, was destined to become the home of Europe's first civilisation, comparable with, and in some respects surpassing, those of Egypt and Mesopotamia. Many, in fact, consider its civilisation, which included cultivation of the land, pastoral farming, writing, city life, metallurgy, a unique architecture and other arts, as one of the most accomplished and inventive the world has known. A. J. Toynbee explained it as the remarkable human response to physical conditions of unusual difficulty, for 'Crete, like the rest of the Aegean world', he stated, 'is bare, barren, rocky, mountainous, and broken into fragments by the estranging sea'. Such a deterministic 'challenge and response' argument, so characteristic of Toynbee, ignored the fact that not only is Crete the largest, it is also the most fruitful and physically varied of the Greek islands and this, together with its traditional function as an important stepping-stone or staging-point between three continents, greatly aided its early progress. Acting initially as 'middleman' in trade between Asia Minor, North Africa, the Levant and the European Mediterranean, the cultural veneers from these areas were interwoven with indigenous Cretan values to produce a civilisation which by 2000BC had reached maturity. Unlike the river-valley civilisations of the Middle East, where nature dictated a certain uniformity, the peculiar geographical conditions of Crete gave a different basis for development. Though the island was centrally controlled, its mountain ranges, steep valleys, isolated plains, upland plateaux and coastal lowlands provided scattered locations in which a village-based agricultural economy complemented urban settlements of a most distinctive type. Protected by their command of the sea, to which they owe their title of the first naval power in history, the Cretans devoted their energies to the refinements of living as the remains of their pleasure palaces illustrate.

The Legends
Something like 2,000 years separated the flowering of the ancient Cretan civilisation from that of the classical era. Not surprisingly, therefore, its recollections by the citizens of fifth– and fourth–century Athens and other city states were dim and

disjointed. Even Homer was of little help, for Crete received only passing mention in his epics, and to Odysseus the island, lying 'amidst the wine-dark sea', was a distant prospect. Crete was described, however, as 'a fair, rich island populous beyond compute with ninety cities', but other than memories of its famed wealth and of Minos its king, who once ruled the seas, the rest of Cretan culture shaded off into the vagueness of myth. As such it remained until the early years of this century and 'knowledge' of the island was confined to little more than stories of the Minotaur, Theseus, the labyrinth and Ariadne's thread, known to all readers of Victorian adventure annuals.

Victorian respectability, however, demanded the abridged or censored versions of these Cretan tales, for King Minos was plagued with a nymphomaniac wife named Pasiphae who, in the best family tradition, had fallen desperately in love, albeit god-willed, with a white bull which Poseidon had sent from the sea for sacrifice. With the help of the legendary inventor Daedulus, who constructed a hollow wooden cow in which to hide, Pasiphae's bizarre desires were satisfied and the fruit of the union was the Minotaur, a monstrous creature with a bull's head on a human body. Daedulus was now called upon to conceal the creature and Pasiphae's disgrace, and he constructed the famous labyrinth, a complicated almost exitless building where, as tribute to Minos, seven youths and maidens from noble Athenian families were regularly sent to satiate the monster's desire. What exactly their fate was is a subject for speculation!

Theseus, prince of Athens and probably embodying some semi-historical figure or event, volunteered as one of the victims and, with the help of Minos' daughter and her famous ball of thread, successfully slew the Minotaur and was guided safely out of the labyrinth. It was Daedulus who had thought of the thread and when imprisoned with his son Icarus his ingenuity again proved equal to the occasion. Making wings of feathers and wax for himself and his son they flew out of Crete, but Icarus disobeyed instructions and flew too near the sun whose burning rays soon melted the wax. He fell into that part of the Aegean Sea near Samos now called Icarian after him and he was buried on the neighbouring island of Icaria. The unscathed Daedalus flew on to the court of King Cocalus in Sicily, hotly pursued by Minos and the Cretan navy. The next sequences in the saga are confused for they culminated in the inglorious death of Minos by the hand of Cocalus' daughter and the complete destruction of the Cretan sea power. The reasons for this are not given and a 'legendary chapter in the pre-history of the eastern Mediterranean ends', writes Leonard Cottrell (*The Bull of Minos*), 'as mysteriously as it began.'

It is, of course, a great danger to interpret these Cretan tales too liberally, but they might signify, in fanciful and romantic form, the supercession of Cretan culture by Aegean civilisation. Certainly they lend some credit to the invasion theory propounded by scholars to account for the final decline of the island empire. On the more detailed level, however, excavations have substantiated to a remarkable degree the basic reliability of the Cretan traditions.

The Discoverers
In 1889, Heinrich Schliemann, fresh from his archaeological triumphs at Troy, Mycenae and Tiryns, visited a large fairly level-topped mound called Kephala, a few kilometres south-east of the Cretan town of Iraklion. Situated at a valley head, shut in by low hills barring any view of the sea, and bounded on the east and south by gullies, only the intuition of Schliemann would have suspected that this was one of the most amazing of archaeological sites. In fairness it must be said that its first discoverer was an aptly named amateur archaeologist from Iraklion, Minos Kalokairinos, who had carried out some preliminary excavations on store houses. Schliemann's dealings with the Turkish authorities to purchase the site were complicated and protracted and a combination of frustration and ill-health forced him to break off negotiations. In March 1898, the Turks, after more than two centuries of occupation, relinquished Crete making it possible for Sir Arthur Evans, an English scholar from Nash Mills near Hemel Hempstead, to acquire and excavate the site. Work began in 1900. Evans, motivated by Schliemann's discoveries at Troy and elsewhere,

had come to Crete for quite another reason; in the words of his sister Joan: 'in the hope of finding a seal impression and a clay tablet, and Time and Chance had led him to discover a civilisation.'

Work on the site was rewarded almost at once by the most outstanding discoveries and it became clear that the mound was a vast, rich and well-preserved palace site covering an area of some six acres. This had to be Knossos, the capital of legendary Minos and of his empire which Evans christened Minoan. From his nearby house and headquarters, appropriately called the Villa Ariadne, he devoted himself to the mammoth task of uncovering and reconstructing Knossos, and other island sites, spending approximately £250,000 of his own money in the course of thirty years. His results were presented to the world in a monumental four-volume publication, *The Palace of Minos* (London 1921–35). When Evans died in 1941, at the age of ninety, he had accomplished something that no man had achieved before – he had discovered and written, on his own, a new chapter in the history of civilisation.

The Palace of Minos

The building complex unearthed by Evans was, in reality, several palaces jumbled together. The site itself had been inhabited at least from Neolithic times but the distinctive Minoan culture belonged to the Cretan Copper and Bronze ages conveniently subdivided today into the more descriptive pre-palatial (2600–2000BC), proto-palatial (2000–1700BC) and neo-palatial (1700–1400BC) periods. Within this long time span phases of great brilliance alternated with phases of stagnation and ultimate destruction. The first palace was probably built around 2000BC and then, following an earthquake, was rebuilt on more luxurious lines after 1700BC. Thus most of the structures on view today belong to the new-palace period which flourished until the civilisation's final decline around 1450–1400BC.

Over 1,300 rooms, arranged in five storeys, made up the palace complex. One room seems to have been added to another on a seemingly haphazard design. At its heart, however, was a great central court around which the vast blocks of buildings were grouped. In addition to being the residence of the royal family and their circle of attendant nobles and functionaries, the palace served as the centre of Minoan religion for there were numerous shrines, small chapels and lustral baths for purification rites. The great complex also housed large magazines for oil jars, stores for equipment and foodstuffs, the commercial and manufacturing quarters, and their administrative adjuncts. The palace also had a drainage and sanitation system probably superior to any known in Europe until the nineteenth century, and certainly superior to most modern Greek towns. The Queen's quarters had its bathroom, complete with clay bathtub, and the lavatory at the end of a corridor had unbelievably modern flush fittings, as well as drains and a sewer. An advanced plumbing system with separate lines for drinking, washing and waste water served other sections of the palace. Further examples of the skills of the Minoan builders can be seen in their liberal use throughout the complex of courtyards, breezeways and lightwells for ventilation and illumination.

In order to present the various building levels and the general complexity of the palace – and, of course to protect it from the elements – Evans undertook a certain amount of reconstruction and restoration work, aided over the years by a qualified staff of archaeologists, architects and artists. Stairways, columns, window casements and walls were rendered in reinforced concrete incorporating, wherever possible, actual remains. Frescoes were also copied before their disintegration and the original fragments, pieced together, are in the Iraklion Museum. Many copies were put up at the site adding enormously to the dramatic effect of Knossos. These reconstructions, however, have been much criticised and disputed, yet without them it would be difficult, if not impossible, for the ordinary visitor to comprehend the Minoan achievement in architecture.

The Minoans combined their technical accomplishments with superb artistic refinements, and their civilisation was one of great elegance, vigour, gaiety and well-being. Pottery of expert craftsmanship, statuettes, drinking vessels, gold pendants and other jewellery, cylinder seals and ivory earrings were some of the palace's luxury items which, along with finds from other sites, form part of the unrivalled collection of Minoan art and artefacts in Iraklion's Archaelogical Museum. Detailed scenes on pottery vessels and a large number of frescoes, impressionistic and abstract, provide important glimpses of everyday life and of the physical appearance of the Minoans. The conventional male has a slim-waisted, broad-shouldered body clothed in an elaborate loin-cloth with a large codpiece, which might suggest sexual pride. Most of the male portraits depict almond-eyed youths with curly hair and adorned with arm, neck, waist and wrist ornaments. The Minoan women, incredibly modern-looking, are shown wearing flounced skirts, puffed sleeves and tight bodices which left their breasts bare. One French archaeologist was led to exclaim in surprise 'des Parisiennes', a name still applied to one striking fresco.

Minoan Religion

These female dress conventions were common to both the palace courtiers and to the statuettes of snake goddesses discovered in temple repositories. The latter were manifestations of the mother or nature goddess, worshipped throughout much of the ancient world at this time, and of which Athena, goddess of Athens, was undoubtedly a descendant. But at Knossos there appears to have been a more important form of cult worship which may have been the basis of the Minotaur legend, certainly this was the opinion of Evans who was eager to relate his discoveries to the traditional stories. Dominating all Cretan mythology and religion was the bull cult and one striking and very famous fresco shows men and women (the Athenian tribute victims, perhaps) exercising themselves in a curious and sinister kind of bull-leaping sport – somersaulting over the back of a charging bull. This feat probably took place in the central courtyard. The bull is depicted in other murals and also appears on cylinder seals, on drinking or sacrificial vessels and on pottery. The symbol of its horns is associated with the double-headed axe in innumerable figurative representations and both may denote the twin-peaked Mount Idha which dominates this central part of Crete and is, itself, clothed in mythology. Perhaps more to the point is the Cretan word for double axe – *labrys* – which in conjunction with the ancient suffix *–nthos* gives *labyrinthos*, 'the house of the double axe'. The complex structure of Knossos, especially to visitors, hostages or tribute victims, might well have gained it the reputation of being an inescapable maze.

Evans had further ideas on the meaning of the bull cult and its probable ritualistic demands. One warm June night, when resting in the Villa Ariadne, he experienced one of Crete's frequent earthquakes; on average about two severe ones occur each century with minor tremors every year. He graphically described the incident in his journal: 'Small objects were thrown about, and a pail, full of water, was splashed nearly empty. The movement, which recalled a ship in a storm, though of only a minute and a quarter's duration, already produced the same physical effect on me as a rough sea. A dull noise rose from the ground like the muffled roar of an angry bull.' Imagination or intuition linked this incident and others with a line Evans recalled from the *Iliad*: 'In bulls does the Earth-shaker delight.' Poseidon, the god of the earthquake, and later of the sea, was associated with the bull in Cretan legend and there are constant references in Homer to his activities; 'Up on high the Father of men and gods thundered ominously, and down below, Poseidon caused the wide-world and the lofty mountain-tops to quake. Every spur and crest of Idha of the many springs was shaken.' The incidence of seismic destruction at Knossos, and elsewhere, was readily apparent from Evans's excavations. Could it be that bull-baiting and worship, and the legends this fostered, were attempts by the Minoans to appease the destructive forces of nature?

Other Minoan sites
Both politically and architecturally the palaces of Phaestos, Mallia and Kato Zakros parallel the development of Knossos.

Occupying a solitary hill commanding the rich Messara plain and towered over by Mount Idha to the north, Phaestos is traditionally associated with Rhadamanthys, the brother of Minos, but how closely it was linked with Knossos is a subject of dispute. Here again the excavation is mainly the achievement of one man, the Italian Frederic Halbherr, but there is no extensive reconstruction, merely the conservation of what remains. The palace had a large central court with an impressive staircase, around which the rooms and quarters, including large magazines, were arranged. Of the finds from the site, now in Iraklion, the most interesting was a round black disc, stamped in hieroglyphics, which appears to have been of religious significance.

The Messara region was obviously favoured by the Minoans and 3km from Phaestos, on the other side of the hill, is the villa of Aghia Triada. This was a prince's residence, the home of a wealthy vassal chieftain or a summer palace of the kings of Phaestos, for in Minoan times the sea came much closer to the villa's grounds. In every respect Aghia Triada is a minor version of the larger palaces and, in spite of its destruction, it still presents an uncommonly elegant appearance, one perfectly adapted to its residential requirements.

On the north coast, 39 kilometres east of Iraklion are the well-preserved ruins of the palace of Mallia. It lies in the shadow of the Lasithi Mountains and is traditionally associated with Sarpedon, another brother of Minos. Unlike Knossos and Phaestos the site is flat, but its plan conforms to these palaces, as does that of Kato Zakros in the extreme east of Crete. This is the latest Minoan palace discovery and excavations began in 1962. It is estimated that the total complex had from 200 to 300 rooms built on two or three levels, and finds from the site indicate that this was a royal centre of considerable commercial importance. Other less important Minoan settlements occur in this part of Crete.

The Minoan palaces were the centres of extensive urban development and vast surrounding areas have yet to be excavated. Scholars' estimates of the population of Knossos, both palace and dependent city, range from 30,000 to 100,000 and ruins stretch considerably beyond those visible from the palace hill. Houses, graves and connecting lanes also surrounded the Phaestos palace, and Mallia had extensive manufacturing and residential quarters. Of all the Minoan sites, however, it is only Gournia that shows the almost complete remains of a provincial town. Situated on a small knoll a short distance from the Gulf of Merabello, it has no references in ancient texts and showed no remains until its excavation between 1901 and 1904. Its small palace was hardly more than a large villa obviously aping its betters, for Gournia was a manufacturing town and its most striking features were a network of narrow paved streets, and closely packed domestic quarters connected by wider lateral avenues. Gournia might well have been a self-supporting and self-governing town, though politically it would have been dependent on the larger palace centres and on the Minoan navy for its trade and protection. In fact, the empire's whole defence system relied on sea power, coastal installations and naval reputation, for the kings were strong enough to leave their palaces unwalled, secure from threats from overseas and, it seems, from each other. Minoan civilisation must be seen, therefore, as an integrated commercial complex rather than as militaristic; its influence extended beyond Crete to other Aegean islands and to settlements established on the coasts of Asia Minor and the Levant. The recently excavated Minoan township on the island of Thera or Santorini, buried under ten feet of pumice and other volcanic material, provides much of the answer to the later history of Minoan Crete.

CRETE AND ATLANTIS

Somewhere around 1450BC the rich civilisation of the Minoans terminated in a sudden and widespread, but rather mysterious disaster. The palaces and other settlements were destroyed simultaneously and subsequently looted, which some authorities attributed to invaders or to rebel forces which attacked and burnt these settlements. The most generally accepted view, however, is that their destruction was caused by the catastrophic explosion of Santorini (ancient Thera), the still active volcanic island 96 kilometres due north of Crete, which was accompanied by a rain of volcanic matter, tidal waves and an earthquake or quakes on Crete itself. Dramatic as this might seem, Crete's earlier archaeological record indicates that previously, around 1700BC, the palaces had been destroyed by some natural disaster. There was no break in continuity, however, and their rebuilding on luxurious lines marked the beginning of the new palace period.

But this second great earthquake was of a totally different magnitude and the gravity of the disaster made a lasting impression on folk memory, taken up centuries later by the tantalisingly short and unfinished tales recorded in Plato's *Critias* and *Timaeus*. These are accounts of Atlantis, that civilised island state overwhelmed by a marine flood of which a garbled account is preserved in Egyptian records. Atlantis was later popularly located west of the Straits of Gibraltar, and confused with the islands of the fabled Hesperides. A descriptive passage in Seneca's *Medea* of a continent beyond the seas is said to have impressed Columbus before his voyage of discovery. The quest for lost Atlantis has inspired an immense literature but, today, the combined results of geological and archaeological scholarship are supportive of earlier held views that the Atlantis legend revolves around the island of Santorini and that its 'disappearance' is a reference to the end of Minoan dominance in the Aegean world.

The volcanic history of Santorini is well documented. Strabo records an eruption in 196BC which lasted for four days and there are records of others in AD727, 1570, 1707, 1866 and 1925. The most serious recent earthquake occurred in July 1956 when 53 people were killed and 2,400 houses destroyed. Some islanders emigrated, but the majority remained and rebuilt their shattered homes and churches in the strong barrel-vaulted roof style so typical of Santorini.

Yet none of this volcanic or seismic activity was remotely comparable with the cataclysmic event at the end of Minoan times which literally blew the heart out of the island which was then some 16 kilometres in diameter and dominated by a cone-shaped summit perhaps 500 to 800 metres in height. Strongili, the Round One, is an ancient name that preserves the memory of what Santorini looked like. Today, it is a group of islands, but the main one, Thera, which is crescent shaped, cannot be disassociated from Therasia and Aspronisi. When viewed on a map or from the air, the circular outline of the group is very clear and it is easy to visualise the outer rim of the once united island and also the inner rim, which now surrounds a great central expanse of sea over 80 square kilometres in extent. At the centre of this sunken caldera the Kaemeni, or Burned Islands, represent the active vents of the volcano and are products of at least eleven phases of activity since prehistoric times. It is estimated that the force of the great Santorini explosion was many times that of Krakatoa in 1883. When it is appreciated that Krakatoa itself generated tidal waves over thirty metres in height the devastation of the coastal areas of Minoan Crete and other Aegean islands can easily be postulated. The Greek myths and legend-histories supply many references to flooding of such coastal plains on both sides of the Aegean. They come from Attica, Rhodes, the Saronic Gulf, the Argolid, Lycia and the Smyrna hinterland, and although these references cannot be firmly dated and might not refer to the same event, as a group they may add up to a genuine memory of the Thera disaster. Circumstantial evidence also indicates that the effects might have been more widely felt and the Old Testament plagues of Egypt have been attributed to volcanic disaster.

The late Greek archaeologist Marinatos was the first to link the destruction of Minoan Crete with Santorini, yet he was unable to investigate his theory until the discovery in 1967 of an extensive Minoan settlement on the island near the village of Akrotiri. Buried and preserved by volcanic material, a township complete with buildings two and three storeys high, squares, shops and workshops was revealed after excavation. Ceramic pots, vases and other finds, now on display in Athens, testify to the high level of culture of the site, and its exquisite frescoes, depicting the manners and customs of its peoples, leave no doubts as to its cultural links with Crete. Of major importance are frescoes of decorative sea-daffodils, which are seen to this day blossoming on the shores of Greece. They come from what is called the 'Room of Women' and their religious significance is indicated by their association with the double axe and the sacred Cretan bull-horns.

Santorini's geology and archaeology continue to be studied in detail and now provide the strongest testimony to the destructiveness of the eruption. But what it did to the island is unimportant when compared to its effect on the Minoanised archipelago surrounding it. 'A brilliant and refined culture,' states J. V. Luce (*The End of Atlantis*), 'floundered under the brutal impact of Theran vulcanism. The tidal waves were the real *bull from the sea* which was sent to plague the rulers of Knossos.'

3

Citadels, States and Wars

With the collapse of ordered existence in Crete, the centre of gravity of the Greek world moved to the mainland, particularly to the Argolid district of the eastern Peloponnesus where a loose federation of states developed under the strong leadership of Mycenae. This transference of power, however, was not a straightforward affair, for extensive cultural and commercial dealings between Crete and mainland Greece had existed for some time, though authorities have differed in their interpretation of the precise relationship. Some maintain that Mycenae was colonised by the Minoans, and others that the mainland rulers remained politically independent but were attracted to the higher civilisation of Crete which they imitated in dress, art and architecture. There is now considerable evidence to suggest, especially towards the end of Minoan times, that the reverse was also the case – mainland reaction on Knossos itself.

One of the capstones in the reconstruction of Greek prehistory was the decipherment by Michael Ventris in 1952 of a peculiar script called Linear B, found on tablets on Knossos and at mainland sites such as Mycenae and Pylos. To the astonishment of the scholarly world Ventris, who by profession was an architect rather than a linguist or archaeologist, proved that this previously unreadable script was an exceedingly archaic form of Greek rather than a non-Hellenic Cretan language as supposed by Evans and others. The suggestion seemed clear; after c1850BC, and in the wake of the Ionians, further Greek-speaking peoples had appeared, the Achaeans, who developed extensive dealings with the Minoans, passing on to them their language and taking Cretan artistry in return. It is almost certain that they conquered Knossos, but whether it

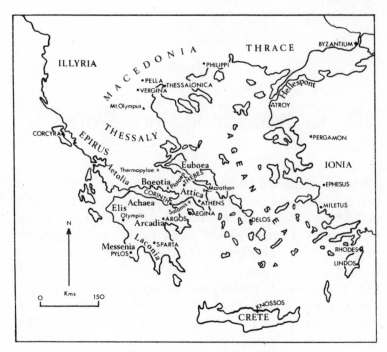

Classical and Hellenistic sites

became subordinate or was independently ruled is not known. Either way the two centres and their dependencies became trading rivals or competitors until the Minoan command of the sea finally passed to the mainland centres.

The Achaeans can be regarded as successful adventurers whose citadels at Mycenae, Tiryns, Pylos, Orchomenus and the Isle of Gla (both in Boeotia), and even the Acropolis of Athens, suggest the existence of a war-minded society with strong feudal characteristics. It was a hybrid civilisation, the fusion of Greek or Achaean restraint and order with Minoan artistry and imagination, and the adjective Mycenaean, with which it is labelled, is taken from its leading political and military centre. Major differences occurred, however, and these are best illustrated in their respective palace centres. Whereas the Cretan palace, seen as a medley of rooms and corridors, appears to have developed naturally, the Mycenaean palace-citadel was conceived in relation to a megaron, a sort of central

Much of the ancient history of Greece is preserved in its archaeological ruins: (*above*) the remains of the fifth-century BC Doric temple, dedicated to Poseidon, stand dramatically on the Sounion promontory at the south-east end of Attica; (*below*) a section of the excavated and partly reconstructed Minoan palace complex of Knossos, near Iraklion in Crete. Its site is connected with some of the most famous mythological stories in antiquity

The feuding city states of classical Greece also recognised certain sites and territories which were neutral and in which truces were upheld. Such was Epidaurus (*left*) whose ancient theatre, with a capacity for 14,000 spectators, is the best preserved in Greece. It lies adjacent to the sanctuary of Asclepios, the God of Healing; the prestige of Delphi (*right*) was related to its famous oracle which attracted visitors from all over the ancient world. The remains of the Tholos, a round Doric temple, are regarded by many as one of the most exquisite monuments of antiquity 'baronial' hall. Its hearth, as in early medieval castles, made it the practical and symbolic focus of palace life, and it was approached via a series of vestibules, broad stairways and ramps, the latter leading directly to the main gate to facilitate the movement of four-horse chariots. In further contrast to the Minoan, the Mycenaean palaces were strongly fortified and were obviously the centres of warlike nobles who created the demand for Minoan fashions. Certainly their art and artefacts – swords and spears with gold and silver inlays, jewellery, gold cups, fine furniture and ceramic wares – were greatly influenced by Cretan styles.

GOLDEN MYCENAE

The Mycenaean period was the Golden Age of heroes – mainly because of the works of Homer – to which the classical Greeks looked back nostalgically with awe, admiration and often amusement. History is again difficult to disentangle from legend, but the epic poems provide graphic accounts of Achaean life and of Mycenaean hegemony over other citadels during the rule of the semi-historical figure Agamemnon. The *Iliad* calls the master of 'well-built Mycenae . . . the town rich in gold', 'the anax of men', portraying him as a kind of quasi-feudal overlord.

Mycenae first excites the imagination as the seat of the fated house of Atreus – descendants of Tantalos and Pelops, themselves accursed for inhumane and bizarre deeds at Olympia. Atreus and his brother Thyestes had taken refuge with King Sthenelos of Mycenae and were subsequently invited to become its rulers. The story is that of Cain and Abel poured into the mould of Greek tragedy for the jealousy between the brothers culminated in the infamous affair between Thyestes and Atreus' wife. In order to seal an apparent reconciliation, Atreus prepared a banquet in honour of Thyestes, but served up three of his young sons as the *entrée*, a trick he had learned from his grandfather Tantalos, who, in a similar feast of appeasement, had served his son Pelops to the gods. The anguished curse of Thyestes on learning of the deed fell not on

Atreus himself but on his children and his children's children, and the misfortunes that ensued are immortalised in a number of classical plays of which the trilogy of Aeschylus, known as the *Oresteia (Agamemnon-Choephori-Eumenides)* is the most famous. It became the basis of such modern literature as T. S. Eliot's *The Family Reunion* (1939) and O'Neill's *Mourning Becomes Electra* (1932).

Atreus was succeeded by his son Agamemnon who, according to the *Iliad*, ruled over the plain of Argos, the territory of the north-eastern part of the Peloponessus, including Corinth, and many of the islands. As pre-eminent ruler in southern Greece he was chosen to lead the Achaeans against Troy and it is on his victorious, though delayed, return that his family troubles start. Having already sacrificed his daughter Iphigenia to appease Artemis and hasten his return to Mycenae, Agamemnon found that his impatient wife Clytemnestra had taken Aigisthos, the son of Thyestes, as her lover. The family tree is complicated for Aigisthos was Thyestes' son by the latter's own daughter Pelopia, who, not surprisingly, in a confused royal court choked with intrigue, murder and incest, decided that suicide was a more attractive option. Aigisthos was Clytemnestra's accomplice in the undignified murder of Agamemnon while in his bath, and of the captive Cassandra, daughter of King Priam of Troy. Clytemnestra herself had been among the spoils of an earlier Mycenaean victory which might account for Homer's charitable portrayal of her as a weak woman led astray by people and circumstances. The classical dramatists, less sympathetic to an unfaithful queen, depict her as a calculating murderess with a double motive for revenge – jealousy of Agamemnon's own infidelity and grief and fury at the sacrifice of her daughter Iphigenia. Agamemnon's death is avenged by his children Electra and Orestes. Aeschylus, Sophocles and Euripides all portray Electra as being fanatically hostile to her mother and the driving force behind Orestes who kills Aegisthos and, as implied by Homer, his mother Clytemnestra.

Aeschylus places the murders and court intrigues at nearby Argos, but a visit to Agamemnon's capital at Mycenae becomes all the more moving, disturbing and sinister, if the mind places the events there. Certainly Schliemann had no doubts as to the location of these stories and Mycenae's record bears the scars of many political upheavals and civil wars. The citadel's very age and its bleak somberness, hardly distinguishing it from the rocks on which it stands, produces a chilling effect which uncompromisingly suggests a blood-stained past.

The Excavations
Pausanias was the last of the ancient authors to mention Mycenae, but though it passed into historical oblivion, its site, unlike Knossos or Troy, was neither forgotten nor completely covered. Throughout the ages its location as an archaeological site was known to scholars and the stone lions (or lionesses) guarding its main gate were always visible to arouse the curiosity of travellers. Their heraldic aspect misled members of a French expedition in 1828 to believe that they formed part of some medieval monument, though nearby villagers retained the memory of hidden treasures, and occasional discoveries, confirming their beliefs, fired the imagination of wealthy foreigners. Towards the end of Turkish rule in Greece the site was the object of pilfering by the purveyors of art treasures, not least Lord Elgin, Lord Sligo and the Pasha of Nauplia. With Greek independence Mycenae was placed under the protection of the Greek Archaeological Society and as early as 1840 the wide courtyard leading to the lion gate was cleared.

The citadel was dramatically brought to the attention of the world by the discoveries of Schliemann whose story is one of success in the pursuit of a lifetime ambition. Born in the north German town of Mecklenberg in 1821, his first job was that of a grocer's assistant. From this he moved on in various professions, and with shrewd and practical business-sense amassed a fortune in Europe and America. Since boyhood Schliemann had possessed an undying passion for Homer and the cities mentioned in the epics and by the age of thirty-three he was the master of fifteen languages including Latin, and Ancient and Modern Greek. With his money behind him he established himself in Greece and the Turkish Aegean, moving to Mycenae after his successful excavations at Troy. Yet Schliemann was petulant and impatient and his first investigation of the site in 1874 lasted only five days, during which thirty-four trenches and pits yielded remains which he considered unimportant. His excavations were continued in 1876, and proceeding into the citadel from the lion gate he discovered in August of that year the royal shaft graves, now known as Grave Circle A. In them were preserved objects of gold, silver, bronze and terracota, and the epic phrase 'Mycenae rich in gold' received a new and real meaning.

Unlike the dedicated Evans at Knossos, Schliemann worked at Mycenae for fourteen years only. Hardly less spectacular, though lacking the glamour in terms of discoveries, was the work on the site by Christos Tsountsas who between 1884 and 1902 brought to light 'Agamemnon's palace', the subterranean cistern, houses within the citadel and a number of chamber and tholos tombs. Then came the turn of the British archaeological school under the supervision of J. B. Wace, and joint efforts by Greek and British excavators have continued to the present. Excavations at Mycenae are today supplemented by extensive restorations and gradually parts of the citadel, particularly its walls, are assuming their original aspect.

The Citadel

Mycenae is situated in the north-west corner of the Argos Plain, a strategic position which controlled the shortest route from Crete and the southern Aegean to central Greece. It occupies a detached spur 278 metres in height and is backed by Mounts Prophitis Ilias and Zara. Deep ravines to the north and south provide it with natural defences which are further strengthened by fortification walls constructed of roughly hewn 'Cyclopean' stone masonry. This is of such large dimensions that the ancient Greeks maintained that only the Cyclops with superhuman powers could have moved and placed them in position. The thickness of the walls ranges from 5·5 to 7·5 metres and though their original height is nowhere preserved it is estimated that they approached 12 metres.

The citadel's main entrance is at the north-west by way of the famous lion gate which is a truly megalithic monument and one of the oldest pieces of monumental sculpture in the western world. It dates from c1250BC and in Mycenaean times it was probably a summary representation of the might of the palace within. The gate is wide enough to take a chariot and is fronted by a narrow court, 15 metres long and 7·25 metres wide, which forced a reduction in numbers of enemy attackers on the main entrance. A smaller gate in the north wall leads to an underground cistern fed by a stream that is invisible outside, a refinement of siege defence that must have saved Mycenae from capture many a time.

The Lion Gate, Mycenae

Within the citadel the road from the lion gate curls up the hill, past the royal graves to the palace at the summit, occupying two terraces connected by a flight of stairs. From this height a clear picture is obtained of the extent of the lower settlement outside the walls with its ancient houses and numerous tombs. The so-called tomb of Clytemnestra is a great domed sepulchral monument whose recently reconstructed roof rises to 13 metres. Its construction of skilfully joined stone blocks in regular layers of gradually smaller rings anticipates the use of the cupola in architecture. Almost adjacent is the

'Tomb of Aigisthos' which presents similar features, but the masterpiece of its kind is the 'Treasury of Atreus' (also called the 'Tomb of Agamemnon') whose massive construction emphasises the power and grandeur of Mycenaean civilisation.

THE DORIANS

By 1400BC Mycenaean influence had spread over the whole of the Aegean and beyond – notably to Cyprus, important for its copper mines. Remains have also been unearthed in the Lipari Islands and manufactured items were traded as far west as Britain. For a further two centuries the mainland palaces with their tributary centres continued to prosper, though not without internal rivalries, some of them on a massive scale. History, archaeology and legend now seem to agree that the siege of Troy took place around 1250 or 1200BC when a large Achaean fleet from all over southern Greece, including Crete, was assembled under the direction of Agamemnon. Ostensibly, the sacking of the great trading city at the entrance to the Dardanelles was to avenge the abduction by Alexander (Paris), Prince of Troy, of Helen the wife of King Menelaus of Sparta, Agamemnon's brother. To Grote the Trojan War, though 'literally believed by the Grecian public' was 'essentially a legend and nothing more'. Yet in this he was again proved wrong, for Schliemann's discovery of Troy (or a series of Troys) substantiated such a naval expedition, which in reality was a political move to break the Trojan's stranglehold on Black Sea trade. Though Mycenae was victorious the Trojan War had been a protracted affair and ultimately it turned out to be disastrous for the Achaean power, which never recovered from the exhaustion which the campaign had involved. This left a profound impression on Greek folk memory and as far as the legends are concerned the death of Agamemnon may be taken as the real start of Mycenaean decline.

The invasion of the Dorians between 1100 and 800BC left an even greater impression on Greek folk memory. They were one of several Greek tribes from the north-western Balkans who for some time had been encroaching on the Greek world. Speaking a harsher and broader variant of the Greek language, the Dorians were in the Iron Age stage of culture and wielded the sword as readily as they used the plough. Not inappropriately the period is named the 'Dark Age', for it was one of violence, pillaging, depopulation and homeless refugees. Under the Dorian impact the Mycenaean palace-bureaucracies disappeared and every citadel in southern Greece, with the exception of Athens, which somehow escaped was plundered and burned. Refugees from the Peloponnesus fled to the mountains or overseas and may have been responsible for the founding of the twelve cities of Ionia on the Asia Minor coast, which included Miletus and Ephesus. On the islands the Dorian invasion was marked by less widespread destruction, probably because there was little organised resistance. On Crete, however, the native population was reduced to a serf class though many took to hill refuges or escaped to the far east of the island where they seem to have kept alive the remnants of their Minoan-Mycenaean heritage.

Much of the Greek world was thus lost to an invading people with a lower cultural level, but ultimately the fusion of opposed forces produced some interesting results. The strong sense of form which the Dorians brought was blended with local art traditions to produce the distinctive geometric-style pottery of Athens and Corinth. But it is on the political front that the Dorian invasion is significant for gradually the various Greek tribes settled down into small independent, and sometimes isolated, communities that formed the basis of what was to become a characteristic Greek institution, the city state.

THE CITY STATES

Ancient Greece never formed a single national entity and when, around 800BC, it emerged from the Dark Age, the country was divided into a mosaic of small political divisions known as *poleis* (singular *polis*) of which city state is an adequate, though not entirely accurate, translation. Each formed a self-governing unit, territorially defined, with its own system of justice, industry, commerce and customs. It has often been said that they exhibited the process of world history in microcosm for they displayed all the apparatus employed by larger states and empires in their relations with one another. Boundaries were fixed, treaties were made, alliances and leagues founded, ambassadors exchanged and war and peace declared. Though potential rivals all were conscious of their common Greek heritage and of a strong sense of cultural unity which found expression in such gatherings as the games at Olympia where all Greeks came to compete. Founded in 776BC, and held every four years, the games were at first local and then pan-Peloponnesian before they developed into a pan-Hellenic festival. A sacred truce permitted warring states to take part and Olympia became an important pacific and diplomatic centre for all Greece. A similar truce was upheld at Delphi whose oracular shrine made it the greatest centre of pilgrimage in the ancient world and the 'common hearth of Greece'.

The beginnings of the city state obviously date from the latter days of Mycenaean rule for in essence its focus was a defensible point, preferably a hill, with an adequate supply of water and agricultural land nearby. The Athenian acropolis possessed all these advantages and was, as previously stated, an early prehistoric citadel. The hill itself, rising to 156 metres above sea level to form an undulating platform (270m long by 156m wide), provided an easily defensible site, and the distance of 8km from the coast of the Saronic Gulf rendered it safe from sudden enemy attacks. The neighbouring Attic plains produced the necessities of life and Phaleron Bay, a natural harbour for beaching the Athenian ships, had the added advantage of being directly visible from the city. By the seventh century BC Athens had advanced from a small citadel community ruled by kings to being the 'capital' of the larger district of Attica and the focus of a considerable population. Undoubtedly it was the unsettled conditions during the Dorian invasions that forced communities to take refuge in or around the fortified acropolis or 'high city' and gradually this became the focal point of local and regional assembly. The Greeks themselves regarded the city state as the product of this synoecism: 'when several villages', wrote Aristotle, 'are united in a single community large enough to be nearly or quite self-sufficing, the state comes into existence.' Local traditions often ascribed the foundation of a city to a single person and in the case of Athens it was the legendary hero, Theseus, who is credited with uniting the independent Attic communities into a single body. Festivals like the Panathenaica and Synoika preserved the memory of this union, while the cults of the various communities were practised on the protecting acropolis under the watchful eye of Athena.

A combination of geographical, historical and economic factors accounted for the precocious development and general character of the Greek *polis*, but perhaps of equal importance was simply the fact that this was the way in which the Greeks liked to live. Then, as now, they revelled in the ideals of politics and willingly accepted all responsibilities of local self-government. From this a community feeling emerged in which the state was regarded as the optimum unit for the conduct of affairs, the administration of justice and the determination of local policy. To preserve collective interest it was felt that the unit should remain small; Plato's ideal was a community of 5,000 inhabitants, and Aristotle thought that each citizen should be able to recognise all others. Though in terms of population and territorial size the majority of city states remained small, inevitably political prestige and commercial pre-eminence led to cities much larger than the philosophical norm. It is estimated that Corinth had a population of around 90,000, but it was Athens that developed as the giant with possibly half of Attica's 300,000 inhabitants living in the city itself. Few other cities exceeded 20,000 inhabitants but, as Thucydides warned, 'the greatness of cities should be estimated by their real power and not by appearances'. Undoubtedly he had Sparta in mind for though it was 'not built continuously' and resembled 'a group of villages', it proved to be one of the most warlike and politically influential of all states.

COLONIES AND COMMERCE

In spite of their manufacturing and trading activities the city states were founded primarily on agriculture and remained largely dependent on it. In many cases, however, population increase outstripped economic resources and a drift to the towns, so common in modern Greece, was equally marked in ancient times. Land hunger also led to the intensification of other Greek traditions – the dependence on sea-faring activities and migration overseas. The period between 770 and 550BC was one of active Greek colonisation, one of the most remarkable resettlement ventures the ancient world had seen.

Throughout the Mediterranean and Black Sea coasts, but particularly in southern Italy and Sicily, colonies from mother cities were planted on coastal sites and islands, often at the expense of native peoples. Colonists set out under a leader (Oikistes) taking with them the religious and political institutions of their homeland – cults, dialect and constitution, etc. In many respects the colony became a replica of the old settlement, but once it was securely established the cord with the mother city was generally cut and though strong emotional ties often continued, the new settlement acquired complete political independence. There are only a few examples of founder cities claiming political rights over colonies. Corinth, for example, had established a large colonial empire and demanded precedence in joint ceremonies with its offspring, regularly sending magistrates and other officials to check on their internal affairs. This, of course, emphasises the other motive for colonial expansion, for Corinth had grown rich on trade with its commercially important satellites. Ultimately, its dictatorial attitude led to a chain of events which was to topple the city states. One of its richest colonies was Corcyra (Corfu), strategically situated at the entrance to the Adriatic. Though it would be misleading to suggest that Corcyra was in any way the real cause of the Peloponnesian War, it was, nonetheless, in its revolt against Corinth, 'the apple of discord' that ultimately led to the great conflict between Athens and Sparta.

Rather than found colonies, Athens tackled its own

economic problems in an entirely different manner. The Attic soils, inherited from prehistoric times, were some of the poorest in Greece and erosion due to soil exhaustion and deforestation had laid to waste large areas of formerly productive land. Largely to appease the discontent of their less fortunate labourers, the landowners appointed as archon Solon (640–560BC), a statesman and legislator, who introduced significant reforms. Serfdom was ended, agriculture reorganised and a commercial economy inaugurated under which corn was received from Mediterranean and Black Sea areas in exchange for oil and wine. This specialisation fostered the manufacturing of jars for storage and transport, and other ceramic products, and to assist commercial expansion the local currency, based on the state-owned Laurion silver and lead mines, was also reformed. The Athenians grew rich and began to embellish their city architecturally.

The main commercial thorn in the Athenians' side was the neighbouring Saronic island of Aegina which Pericles ungraciously, and with obvious envy, christened 'the eyesore of Piraeus'. Now a popular Athenian resort, in the sixth century it was one of the most flourishing and powerful states in Greece. Well placed for trade between the Peloponnesus, Corinth and central Greece, the Aeginetans also operated overseas commerce with southern Italy, Egypt and the Black Sea lands where they founded colonies. Their currency in copper and iron coins was accepted throughout the ancient world as was their system of weights and measures. In 455BC Aegina fell to Athens but an earlier war, when the Aeginetans succeeded in destroying the Athenian fleet at Phaleron, had awakened Athens to a greater maritime danger, that of Persian expansion in the eastern Mediterranean which threatened the entire independence of the city states.

THE PERSIAN WARS

As early as 546BC the commercial Greek cities of Ionia had fallen to the Persians, whose vast empire during the reign of Darius the Great stretched from the Aegean Sea to the river

Indus. In 499BC Aristagoras led the Ionian cities in revolt, an event which had far-reaching effects on the Greek mainland. Appeals for help brought responses from Eretria, on the south coast of Euboea, and from Athens, with the latter providing twenty ships which took part in the Greek sacking of Sardis. Determined on revenge, Darius despatched a huge army and a fleet of transports to destroy Eretria and in August or September 490BC his forces were intent on marching on Athens, first disembarking in the Bay of Marathon. In what must be one of the most famous battles in history, the Persians, after a short engagement, were routed by a small Athenian force and a contingent of Plataeans, collectively under the command of Miltiades. According to tradition 6,000 Persians fell in the battle as against only 192 Greeks. Militarily Marathon was of small importance but its effects on Greek morale was enormous. 'These were the first Greeks', says Herodotus, 'who had the courage to face up to Persian dress and the men who wore it, whereas up to that time the very name of the Persians brought terror to a Greek.'

Ten years later Darius' son and successor, Xerxes, despatched another expedition against Greece. This time the Persian army came by land through Macedonia, and the fleet sailed along the Aegean coast. In an equally dramatic battle at the pass of Thermopylae, near Lamia, Leonidas, having dismissed the greater part of the Greek forces, remained with his 300 Spartans to slow down the Persian advance. But the heroic resistance was soon overcome and the Persians moved on to Athens, burning the city and sacking the acropolis. The Athenians had already fled, having moved their families to Aegina, Salamis and the Argolid coast. The Greek fleet, more than half of which was Athenian, lay in the Straits of Salamis under the shadow of the island's acropolis and it was in this narrow expanse of water on 27 or 28 September 480BC that the independence of Greece from Persian rule was assured. On approaching the Straits from Phaleron Bay the mighty Persian fleet was outmanoeuvred by Athenian triremes and many of its ships were destroyed. The remainder retreated across the Aegean where they were again successfully challenged near

Miletus, thus freeing a large part of Greek Asia Minor from Persian control. Xerxes was forced to leave his land army under the command of Mardonius and this too, in the following year, was defeated by a confederate army near Plataea in Boeotia. Salamis and Plataea were decisive battles and the Persian menace was effectively removed.

ATHENS' GOLDEN AGE

The period covered by the Persian Wars was a formative one in the history of the Greek city states for a political pattern had emerged which was effectively to characterise Greece for a number of centuries. The major cities of Athens, Sparta, Thebes, Corinth and Argos had each acquired political and cultural individuality and the subsequent history of the states was largely that of the interrelationships of these five. Athens, however, had gained great prestige from the Persian wars and exploited its position to transform the defensive alliance that had existed against the Persian threat into its own personal empire. This often meant the employment of force against member cities reluctant to pay tribute to the common treasury, whose headquarters was initially the central Cycladic island state of Delos, before it was removed to Athens in 454BC for security. Within a short time after the Persian Wars, therefore, Athens, financed by tribute and trade, reached the acme of economic and cultural supremacy, boasting also a fully developed political system. The latter had been perfected by Pericles, the general and statesman in control of Athenian affairs from about 460BC until his death from plague in 429 BC. 'Ours is a Constitution', he stated, 'which does not imitate those of others, but rather sets them an example. Its name, because it rests not with a few but with the majority, is Democracy.'

Economic and physical reconstruction had been an Athenian prerequisite and the major need for an enlarged shipbuilding industry and a strong merchant marine, consequent to the rapid increase in trade, led to the planning and building of the new port city at Piraeus. The suggestion to develop the rocky, spur-shaped promontory with its deep natural harbours came from Themistocles, the commander at Salamis and the founder of the Athenian navy. In fact, the sacking of Phaleron by the Aeginetans had made a new defensive port a matter of some urgency. The plan was for two walled cities – Athens and Piraeus – 8km apart, each with fortifications about 11km in circuit and with protective communications formed by the famous Long Walls. In theory these turned city and port into a single fortress making it possible for Athens to bring in supplies even during wartime.

Themistocles was banished, for political reasons, before his plans came to fruition but the building and reconstruction work was taken over by Pericles whose domestic policy was dependent on an extension of maritime commerce. In a planning sense the distinguishing feature of Piraeus was not so much its naval establishments and strong defences, but the detailed and regular layout of its street pattern and public buildings which is attributed to Hippodamus, an architect-planner from Miletus. Through the new view of preconceived planning, already successfully adopted in a number of colonial cities, he made Piraeus the model city of the Greek mainland and one whose axial-grid street pattern contrasted strongly with that of Athens whose narrow and irregular streets were the product of natural and often haphazard growth.

Contrary to popular conception, Athens was never a planned city though, like the majority of old established Greek centres, it consisted of two distinct units. The first, the acropolis or high city, was the original nucleus which had formerly housed the citadel of its early rulers. When Athens was strengthened by a circuit of walls the acropolis lost some of its initial usefulness in defence and developed increasingly as the city's religious and ceremonial centre. Surrounding the acropolis was the second unit, the asty or lower town, which comprised a number of manufacturing and residential districts focusing on the agora, the general meeting-place and centre of public life. The principal urban roads and country highways, via Athens' thirteen gates converged on the agora and it was graced by many monumental buildings. Long colonnades or stoas offered

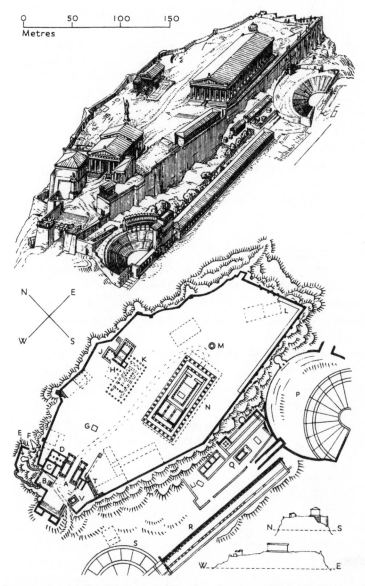

0   50   100   150

Metres

Reconstruction and plan of the acropolis (Based on drawings of H. Luckenbach and Sir Banister Fletcher):

A–Propylaea; B–Pedestal of Agrippa; C–Pinacotheca; D–Roman cistern; E–Clepsydra; F–Caves of Apollo and Pan; G–Statue of Athena Promachus; H–Sacred olive tree; J–Erechtheum; K–Old temple of Athena; L–Platform for votive statues; M–Roman temple; N–Parthenon; P–Theatre of Dionysus; Q–Aesculapium; R–Stoa of Eumenes; S–Odeum of Herodes Atticus; T–Mycenaean wall; V–Temple of Athena of Victory shade in summer and protection from rain in winter to the throng of people who transacted the day-to-day business of the city, met for political and social discussions or to hear and exchange the rumours and gossip of a market place.

Art and Architecture

For Athens the Periclean age was one of great creative achievement, the Golden Age in which architects, sculptors, writers and thinkers produced works of art and literature that became the inspiration of later times. To Pericles Athens was the 'school of Greece'; 'Our city', stated Isocrates in his eulogy of Athens, 'has surpassed all people of the world in eloquence and philosophy.' One of the preoccupations of Pericles was the adornment of the acropolis with imperishable works of art and he entrusted the construction of the Propylaea, its grandiose gateway, to Mnesicles, a fashionable architect of the time. Built entirely of Pentelic marble in the Doric style, it was completed in five years and extended across the western front of the acropolis, the whole structure forming an imposing vestibule with five gates through which the sanctuary was entered. In its north wing was the Pinacotheca which according to Pausanias was a small room used for exhibiting pictures, while to the south of the main gate the small Ionic temple of Nike Apteros or Athena of Victory, now restored, commemorated the Greek victories over the Persians. Its frieze, which runs round the whole of the exterior, represents Greek and Persian in combat.

The main building of the acropolis, however, is the Parthenon, the temple of the virgin goddess Athena, the guardian of Athens. It stands on the foundations of an earlier shrine (also to Athena). Its architects Ictinos and Callicrates succeeded, again through the medium of Pentelic marble, in producing the most perfect specimen of Doric proportion and refinement. The sculptures on the pediments were the work of Phidias, or of his school, as was the frieze around the sanctuary proper which represented in low relief the various stages of the procession of the Panathenaica, the great festival held annually in honour of the goddess. Phidias also created the 12m statue of Athena which dominated the Parthenon's hall. Made of

A scene in the Plaka, the old district of Athens. Though much of it is now given over to tourism, or to the archaeologists, its old houses still retain the character of the nineteenth century town

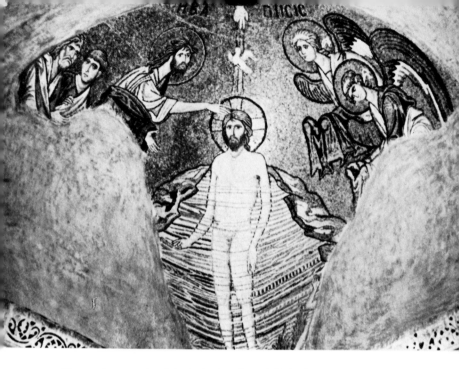

Contrasting mosaics: (*above*) the baptism of Christ from the eleventh century Monastery of Daphni, near Athens;* (*below*): Dionysios seated on a panther, from the House of the Masks in Delos. This mosaic masterpiece must have been commissioned for some great and influential Hellenistic master

ivory and gold over a wooden core it is thought to have been destroyed some time in the fifth century AD.

Many of the Parthenon's sculptures were removed in 1801 by Lord Elgin, then British ambassador at Constantinople, and taken to Britain where they remain as one of the principal showpieces of the British Museum. This action was as much an act of salvage as of vandalism for the destruction of the building and the stripping of its treasures goes back at least to the seventeenth century, and little attempt was made by the Turkish authorities to preserve what remained. By the end of the eighteenth century it was really a battle between France and Britain and the Comte de Choiseul-Gouffier, a French diplomat and ardent philhellene, instructed his agent in Greece 'to lose no opportunity of pillaging Athens'. Thus a sizeable piece of the Parthenon, and other Greek treasures, has gravitated to the Louvre.

The Parthenon, especially during the Peloponnesian War, was as much a national treasury as a place of worship, but although the symbol of Athenian pride and unity it never supplanted the adjacent Erechtheion as a national shrine. The latter's roots went deep into the legendary history of the city as the site of the contest between Athena and Poseidon and as the burial place of Athena's ward Erechtheus. The surviving temple, in the Ionic style, has a unique architectural feature on its south side – a porch with six draped female figures, the Caryatids, serving as roof supports. One is a copy, the original being in the British Museum along with one Ionic column, the depredatory work again of Lord Elgin.

Athens may have contained some of the outstanding examples of architecture and sculpture, but building activity of this kind was widespread in Greece in the fifth and fourth centuries BC. The great temple of Zeus at Olympia, those at Sounion and Aegina and the various temples at Delphi and elsewhere are all exquisite examples of the artistic and architectural genre of the age. Sculptors as well as builders were in heavy demand throughout the Greek world and at Olympia Phidias was commissioned to execute the colossal gold and ivory statue of Zeus. Myron, Polycletus, Praxiteles

Temple of Olympian Zeus, Athens

and Lysippus were other important sculptors whose bronze and marble figures of gods, athletes and lesser mortals adorned both public places and private residences. Many of Greece's ancient theatres also belong to this period; that at Epidaurus, capable of accomodating 16,000 spectators, is one of the most noteworthy. The theatre of Dionysios at the foot of the Athenian acropolis was of similar capacity.

Literature and Science
The great flowering of architecture and sculpture was paralleled in the field of literature by the works of poets, dramatists, philosophers and historians, all of which were initially influenced by the works of Homer. The Greeks regarded Pindar (*c*518–438BC) as their major poet. Born in Boeotia and educated in Athens, he was the master of the lyric ode, composing among other things choral songs in honour of victories in the Olympic and other games. Taking the form of a thanksgiving and infused with deep religious feeling, they were intended for recitation in the home cities of the victors.

The great dramatists of the classical age were Aeschylus, Sophocles, Euripides and Aristophanes, whose combined works are conceded to be the world's finest body of dramatic literature. Whereas the first three were tragedians,

Aristophanes was most admired for his comedies which perfectly complemented the serious tone of the works of his contemporaries. Forty-four of their plays have survived though this number is obviously incomplete; Sophocles alone is credited with over one hundred.

Greek prose developed with the teachers of rhetoric and oratory; speeches delivered either in the Assembly or in the courts of law were elaborately prepared and, of necessity, persuasive in their appeal. The speeches of Isocrates, Demosthenes and Lysias were eloquent and dexterous, but it was the historians who became the real masters of prose writing, grouping facts and ideas around a central theme and applying the principles of literary criticism. Herodotus is regarded as the father of history (and also of lies!), but it is Thucydides' *History of the Peloponnesian War* which is the real masterpiece, especially when it is realised that his material had to be laboriously collected by word of mouth.

In that age of inquiry philosophy made an irresistible appeal. Of the writings of Socrates little has survived, though the works of Plato range from ordinary simple conversations to the most inspired flights of fantasy. But it was Aristotle, more strictly a philosopher and scientist of Hellenistic rather than classical times, who left the greatest mark. His works on ethics, science, politics and metaphysics must place him amongst the greatest thinkers of all time. Yet there were other masterminds, too numerous to mention, who were instrumental in placing Greece in the foreground of developments in all branches of knowledge, opening up broad horizons in such disciplines as mathematics, astronomy, medical science, physics, biology and mechanics.

THE PELOPONNESIAN WAR

The period of Athenian greatness was short lived. In 405BC, only seventy-five years after the battle of Salamis, the Athenians suffered defeat at the hands of the Spartans and an age of political eclipse set in. The defeat was the culmination of the cruel and protracted conflict known as the Peloponnesian

War which began in 431 BC and lasted for twenty-seven years.

The Spartans were traditional enemies of the Athenians for, in both character and ideals, the two peoples had little in common. A military state from the beginning, Sparta's organisation on a warlike basis was attributed to Lycurgus whose laws were interpreted with increasing stringency with the passing of time. By the fifth century a totalitarian and militaristic constitution enforced a ruthlessly austere way of life, the worst features of which were the oppression of its subject peoples and, not unknown to the modern Greeks, an all-powerful secret police. Its citizens were allowed only one meal a day, its boys, taken from their parents at an early age, were submitted to the most arduous forms of training without parallel in history, and the regime enforced contempt of wealth, luxury, beauty and art. Sparta kept its doors closed to all outsiders and, not surprisingly, it held a peculiar fascination for Greek philosophers and political thinkers.

In many ways war between the states was inevitable, for it escalated, as most wars do, from petty rivalries – in this case from jealousy on the part of Corinth and Megara, the main commercial rivals of Athens, of the latter's power, wealth and prestige especially among the colonies of the west, such as Corcyra, which Corinth still regarded as her own. Persuading the Spartans to engage in a struggle with Athens was a political and military move which involved most of the city states for basically it became a conflict between the Athenian empire (the successor of the Delian League) and Sparta's looser confederation, the Peloponnesian League. In practical terms the struggle exemplified, on a small scale, how a war waged between a maritime and a 'continental' power tends to be conducted, for Sparta with a weak navy was obliged to avoid large-scale engagements at sea, whereas Athens with only a small land army favoured those theatres of combat in which its navy could most effectively damage Spartan interests.

A detailed description of the war's main stages has been left by Thucydides, himself a participant on the side of Athens. The first stage was militarily indecisive, but included the ravaging of Athens by a great plague in which Pericles perished. The second stage ended in 413BC with the defeat of the Athenian expedition to Syracuse in Sicily, a disaster which proved irreparable, though a third stage lasting ten years followed before Athens was forced, by famine, to surrender to Sparta's blockade. Its fleet had already been surprised and destroyed by the Spartan commander Lysander at Aegospotami on the Hellespont. Treachery was another factor in the Athenian downfall.

The protracted war, which brought material devastation, also had grave and deleterious effects on the character and internal life of the city states. The Athenians, now greatly influenced by the oligarchs and by the ambitions of Alcibiades, finally lost confidence in the ideal of democracy and placed absolute power in the hands of thirty men, the Tyrants, whose year-long reign of terror was long remembered. Some 1,500 Athenians were said to have been executed and many more were exiled or fled the city. Further spiritual bankruptcy was revealed in 399BC by the execution of Socrates for an alleged crime of treason. Nothing could have been further from the truth for the great philosopher was devoted to Athens and had also proved himself an especially brave and honoured soldier.

In the years following the Peloponnesian War the individualism of the city states became more pronounced and, in spite of propaganda in favour of the pan-Hellenic ideal, the rivalries between them remained intense. In addition, political faction within the cities endangered the life of the state and paved the way for total decline. 'The race of Hellenes is free', wrote Aristotle, 'and capable of ruling over all if only under one Government.' Such a government was to come from alien powers siezing the opportunities for conquest offered by the confused and politically fragmented Greece. 'In to the vacuum thus created', writes Alexander Eliot, 'Greece subsided to the fretful slumber of a state enslaved.'

4

A Province of Empires

When political unification came to Greece it was the result of foreign domination and for something like two thousand years – up until the nineteenth century, in fact – Greece was destined to play a more subdued, generally provincial role within the confines of larger and more powerful empires. Greek civilisation, as portrayed in the classical city states, was first engulfed by a rising northern power centred on what is now known as western Macedonia, an area of more continental proportions which had hitherto lagged behind the development of southern Greece and had played but a small part in general Hellenic affairs. Though enclosing the Aegean basin, the city states had barely penetrated northern Greece, for Macedonia with its Balkan rather than Mediterranean climate and sparsity of safe anchorages, proved less attractive to a commercially minded and sea-orientated society. In the northern Aegean, colonies of the southern cities were concentrated in tight clusters around the multi-pronged Chalcidice peninsula and on either side of the Hellespont, but many must have numbered their population in hundreds rather than thousands, making them easy targets for Macedonian expansion.

The problem of whether the Macedonians were Greeks has been endlessly debated from the time of Herodotus. They were regarded as 'barbarians' by the southern Greeks who also, rather misguidedly in view of recent archaeological discoveries, perpetuated their image as one of a savage, unsophisticated people. It seems certain that both Achaean and Dorian Greek stock existed in Macedonia which was mingled with fair-headed Illyrian peoples (the root-stock of the modern Albanians), Thracians and some Celts. In a predominantly agricultural environment this hybrid population was initially divided into tribes and clans under the authority of large land-holding chiefs. Below them lived a theoretically free peasantry and over all stood the king exercising, in true feudal manner, military, judicial and even religious powers. The preservation of this type of 'Homeric' monarchy, which paralleled that of the Persian empire, distinguished Macedonia from the city states. It was also the mark of its national unity for, in the face of constant threats from the north and east, strong military leadership was a necessity and the Macedonian rulers were first and foremost warlords.

Several kings bore the title Philip, but it was the shrewd and tenacious Philip II who became most celebrated. Contrary to criticisms emanating from Athens and elsewhere he was no rude and unschooled barbarian, but emphatically a man who valued Greek education and culture and knew how to appropriate it for himself and his descendants. Alexander, his son by Olympias, was tutored for a short time by Aristotle and brought up in the court at Pella where the plays of Euripides were regularly performed and where some of the greatest artists of Greece, including Apelles, Zeuxis and Polygnotos, had worked on the decoration of palace and city. Apelles became the official painter of the Macedonian court and glowing descriptions of his works survive from the ancient writers who thought him the greatest painter of his age.

Pella, formerly connected by a navigable lagoon with the Thermaic Gulf, had replaced Edessa (89km north-west of Thessalonica) as the seat of Macedonian government. It probably remained the capital throughout the height of Macedonia's greatness and chance finds in 1957 located the exact site of the city, estimated to have occupied 2·5 sq km. Excavations revealed a group of opulent buildings, undoubtedly the palace complex of the kings, whose celebrated mosaics are the principal attraction of the site. But the real measure of Macedonia's wealth and artistic attainment comes from a series of major archaeological discoveries – regarded as some of the most important in modern times – at the small village of Vergina near Veria. Systematically studied by the Greek

Archaeological Society since 1937, and the life-long work of Professor Manolis Andronicos, a tomb, opened in 1977, revealed fabulous riches which were obviously not the burial goods of a common man. A diadem and other accoutrements of 'royalty' in gold, a shield of bronze, gold and ivory, silver vases and, resting within a marble sarcophagus, a solid gold burial casket, weighing 24 pounds and embossed with the sun-burst star, the symbol of Macedonian rule, were some of the principal artefacts. Clay pots date the tomb to 350–325BC and Andronicos attributes it to Philip II who would have been the only king buried in Macedonia at this time. There are other clues to the tomb's identity. Classical texts relate that Philip II walked with a limp, the result of a battle wound, and the discovery of a pair of greaves or leg-guards, one slightly shorter than the other is circumstantial evidence in the best archaeological tradition. Another clue lies in a collection of exquisitely carved ivory portraits, one of which bears a marked resemblance to an existing image on a medallion which is believed to be Philip, and one is unquestionably a likeness of Alexander the Great himself. Of Vergina's hundreds of burial mounds, many have been robbed over the centuries, but others have yielded iron swords, bronze ornaments, jewellery, and items of pottery, providing scholars invaluable insights into the art, rituals and customs of ancient Macedonia. Adjacent to 'Philip's tomb' is a smaller burial chamber of particular importance because it contains examples of wall-paintings which are probably the works of Nikomarchos an accomplished painter of the fourth century BC. One depicts the rape of Persephone by Pluto, and the Roman scholar Pliny refers to Nikomarchos as having painted this same subject elsewhere. Subsequent work at Vergina will obviously further contribute to an understanding of ancient Macedonia which is now acknowledged as being a nation rich in art forms as well as proficient in the tactics of war.

GREATER GREECE

Macedonia's wealth in precious metals and other natural resources – greater than those of any of the cities to the south – was the result of military conquest and territorial expansion. This was part of Philip II's plan for the consolidation of the north and early in his reign (359–336BC) he drove the Illyrians from Macedonia, founded a new defensive town, Philippi, on the Thracian marches and extended his control south into Thessaly. His military strength was based on a highly trained professional army which had gained considerable experience from constant skirmishes with both Illyrians and Thracians. The confused politics and divisions of southern Greece also provided ample opportunity for interference and with threats and bribes he skilfully and advantageously exploited the dissensions between the city states.

Demosthenes in his brilliantly rhetorical orations tried, unsuccessfully, to rouse the Athenians against the Macedonian danger. He regarded Philip as a menace to democratic liberty, though others, including Isocrates, saw him as a potential leader of a Greece united against Persia, the traditional enemy. This, in fact, was Philip's major ambition and in 338BC, with Alexander fighting at his side, he forced the issue at the Battle of Chaeronea in Boeotia where the combined Theban-Athenian army was crushed by the unquestioned supremacy of Macedonia. The states of Greece were forcibly enrolled in a pan-Hellenic league that took its orders from Philip and a year later at the congress or synedrion of Corinth Philip's leadership was ratified and a combined crusade against Persia was proclaimed. In the midst of preparations, however, Philip was assassinated and it was Alexander, with a highly efficient expeditionary force at his disposal, who took up the challenge of world conquest.

Alexander, twenty years old when he inherited the Macedonian throne, was already well trained for, and familiar with, the demands of his future, and accounts of his victorious marches read almost like a legend. The Greek historian Arrian in the second century AD provides one of the earliest accounts of Alexander's campaigns and his *Anabasis*, based on contemporary records, also provides a valuable study of the young general's character and personality:

> His body was beautiful and well-proportioned; his mind brisk and active; his courage wonderful. He was strong enough to undergo hardships, and willing to meet dangers; ever ambitious of glory and a strict observer of religious duties. As to those pleasures which regard the body, he showed himself indifferent; as to the desires of the mind insatiable . . . in marshalling, training and governing an army he was thoroughly skilled and famous for exciting his soldiers with courage and animating them with hopes of success, as also in dispelling their private fears by his own example of magnanimity.

Not surprisingly, the name of Alexander passed into the legendary cycles of medieval Europe and to the Greeks, who adulate success and masculine prowess, he remains the most popular folk hero receiving more than slight deification.

Alexander's first aim was to maintain Macedonia's dominant position in Greece for the southern states had attempted to reassert their independence. The revolt of Thebes was ruthlessly suppressed and the city was reported as being completely destroyed except for its temples and one solitary dwelling, the supposed birthplace of the lyric poet Pindar, whose work Alexander admired. The fate of Thebes, where 6,000 inhabitants were killed and 30,000 enslaved, had a sobering influence on the other city states who promptly sent envoys to pacify Alexander and to testify to their loyalty. Multi-faced Athens sent ten, to congratulate him on his punishment of the Thebans for their 'revolutionary spirit', and it might have been this submission that saved the city, though perhaps it was Alexander's respect for his old tutor Aristotle, who had again settled in Athens to teach at its Lyceum.

Having made Greek subjection sure, Alexander turned his attention eastwards and the account of his conquests, whereby his invincible Macedonian phalanx overcame and annexed the Persian empire, swept victoriously over the Indian Punjab and converted Anatolia, Syria and Egypt into Greek colonial states, really belongs to the history of lands other than Greece. The first *Book of the Maccabees* describes briefly how 'he went through to the ends of the earth' and this rapid advance into Asia was halted only by his army's refusal to march any further. Within twelve years Alexander had created the largest empire the ancient world had yet seen, founding numerous cities of which twenty-five are known, including Bucephalia in India, named after his favourite horse – presumably when he grew tired of naming them after himself. Some of these cities, initially strategic military colonies, failed to survive, whereas others, like the Egyptian Alexandria, are sound testimony of the conqueror's shrewd perception of geographical values.

Taking up residence in Babylon, Alexander reigned for a brief period in the manner of an oriental sovereign, even insisting on being considered a son of a god, a style far removed from the traditional Greek values that had motivated his campaign. He died of fever in Babylon in 323BC at the age of 32 and his body, wrapped in gold, is said to have been brought to Alexandria and buried in a glass coffin in a vast tomb at the centre of the city. Its site has never been located, though many rumours have persisted that his body has been seen, still intact, in some underground chamber!

Following his death, Alexander's empire fell apart, for the absence of a capable royal successor resulted in political power devolving on the generals in the provinces. In little more than a decade these generals had become kings of warring states whose boundaries were roughly carved along continental lines. Ptolemy created a Greek kingdom in Egypt centred on Alexandria; Seleucus had a kingdom in Asia with its capital first at Seleucia, then at Antioch; Lysimarchus held Thrace; Antigonus governed Syria and Anatolia; and Cassander controlled Macedonia from a city, formed in 316BC, taking its name Thessalonikeia (in Strabo's spelling) from his wife who was half-sister to Alexander. Cassander maintained a precarious influence over the Greek city states which had reacquired varying degrees of freedom. As before, they regarded themselves as self-contained units, their citizens still endlessly debating and legislating, and forming coalitions or leagues against Macedonian interference. The role they now played, however, even collectively, was an insignificant one, for with little strength compared to the powers of the kings, a united front was seldom achieved. For a time Ptolemaic Egypt dominated the Aegean archipelago, but Macedonia claimed control of the Greek mainland which was to become a battleground for stronger powers. In the course of this confused history Athens was twice occupied by Macedonian troops, once in the year after Alexander's death and again in 262BC when the city took the wrong side in a dispute for the Macedonian throne. Such conflicts and rivalry for the succession left Macedonia considerably weaker than it had been in Philip's day, but for another century or so it maintained its shaken dominance in Greece.

Hellenistic Civilisation

Interwoven with the political tale of division and decline following Alexander's death is a success story involving the economic and cultural triumph of Hellenism in which Greek ideas, as a result of conquest, were spread to an area extending virtually from the Danube to the Indus. Alexander's objective was the cultural union of east and west or the amalgamation of Macedonians, Greeks and Persians, peoples he regarded as the master 'races'. His marriage to Roxane, the daughter of a Sogdian chief, and the mass marriage of his troops to local women at Susa, were practical and demonstrative steps towards this union of peoples. Yet though Greek speech was raised to the position of a universal language and Greek ideas became important factors in the political and religious history of the East, Greek civilisation itself underwent modifications, assuming both a new character and a more universal appeal – a cosmopolitanism in art, literature, philosophy and science which was no longer bounded by the provincial rivalries of the city states.

Culturally as well as politically many of the Greek cities suffered from their inclusion within large empires. Creative power drained away eastwards where brilliant new centres developed at Antioch, Alexandria, Pergamon, Ephesus and Rhodes. The first two were the major commercial cities of the

East and Alexandria, the greatest centre for the Greek dispersal, was also the chief centre for Greek learning in the ancient world. Rhodes, too, in Hellenistic times was a veritable intellectual metropolis christened the 'Second Athens', and its schools of sculpture, painting, literature and oratory had high reputations. Yet the cultural prestige of Athens, particularly in the field of philosophy, also remained high and the city and its sanctuaries received offerings and embellishments from the Hellenistic sovereigns. The Egyptian Ptolemies built a great gymnasium and Eumenes and Attalus, both rulers of Pergamon, built stoas or colonnades as tributes to the ancient centre of Greek culture which, politically, had seen better days. The Stoa of Attalus in the ancient agora was destroyed in 267AD and its stones were used in the construction of a new defensive wall. It was restored by the American School of Classical Studies between 1954 and 1958 and though still not mellowed with age, the long covered colonnade, on to which shops open, illustrates the adaptation of Greek architecture to both climate and purpose.

THE PAX ROMANA

Rome had no positive eastern policy in the Mediterranean until after 200 BC and its initial involvement in Greek affairs was gradual and fortuitous rather than the outcome of a conscious political design to expand its boundaries. The Romans were drawn into the complicated world of the successor states of Alexander's empire by the hostility of Philip V of Macedonia and by appeals for aid and protection from the city states which had themselves formed a defensive coalition known as the Achaean League. In 215BC, during the Second Punic War between Rome and Carthage, Philip took the misguided step of allying himself with the Carthaginian general Hannibal. This provided the Romans with the necessary excuse for intervention in Greece and in the second of the three Macedonian Wars which followed, Philip was defeated (197 BC) and the victorious Roman consul Flamininus, at a ceremony at Isthmia near Corinth, declared Rome the 'protector of Greek freedom'. The defeat of Philip's son Perseus at Pynda in 168BC marked the complete subjugation of Macedonia which in 148BC became a Roman province. Its chief city was Thessalonica whose geographical position in relation to the southern Balkans and the Aegean favoured its development, which was further accelerated by the building of the Via Egnatia, the great military and commercial highway linking the Adriatic with the Greek colony of Byzantium (subsequently Constantinople) on the Bosporus. The road was systematised to form, with the Via Appia, a direct link between Rome and the east by way of Brundusium (Brindisi) and Dyrrachium (Durazzo), and colonies and inns were established with regularity along its course.

The Pax Romana brought mixed blessings to southern Greece. At first the city states were subordinated to Macedonia, though subsequently Augustus (Octavian) separated them into the province of Achaea with its capital at Corinth. This was a new Corinth for earlier, in 146BC, the city had revolted against Roman control and had been mercilessly levelled by the Roman consul Mummius and his ten legates. Athens, however, had played no prominent part in resisting the Romans and was generously treated, initially enjoying peace and a nominal independence. But this was disturbed in 88BC when the city unwisely supported Mithridates, King of Pontus in Asia Minor, in his conflict with Rome. The city's destruction, and that of Piraeus, by the hand of Sulla was almost as complete as its earlier razing by the Persians: fortifications were destroyed, treasures looted and all administrative privileges curtailed. Thereafter Athens and Greece generally, impotent in politics and war alike, were scarcely affected by the wider events of Roman policy, though two civil wars were fought on Greek soil and in Greek waters in which many Greek cities took sides. The first involved Pompey's struggle with Caesar and ended with the latter's victory at Pharsalus in Thessaly in 48BC; the second was the struggle between Mark Antony and Octavian when in 31BC the Emperor was triumphant in the great naval battle off the west coast of Greece near Actium. Individual cities received severe punishments depending on their allegiances and Strabo, visiting Greece two years after Actium, paints a melancholy picture of a desolate countryside with many notable cities in ruins.

Although the Athenians had backed the losers in the civil wars they were generously pardoned in consideration of the past greatness of their city and henceforward they lived chiefly on this reputation. As Roman interest in Greek culture increased, the city attracted an ever increasing number of visitors and its schools were frequented by countless young Romans of good families. A stay in Athens was the nearest equivalent of a period of study at a university and Horace describes his studies there, as does Cicero's son Marcos, though like many students he was complacent about the great centre of learning.

The Emperor Hadrian's affection for Athens was displayed in the building programme he inaugurated. He presented the city with a library, a pantheon and a gymnasium; he built a temple dedicated to Hera, repaired the theatre of Dionysios and completed the temple of Olympian Zeus which was begun by Peisistratos more than six centuries earlier and had provided Sulla with rich spoil. The magnificent building with 104 Corinthian columns (16 survive) formed the nucleus of the 'new Athens' or Hadrianopolis, a quarter laid out to the east of the old city and entered through a triumphal archway which still stands. The arch has identical façades, except for the inscriptions: that on the south-east side reads, 'This is Athens the ancient city of Theseus'; that on the north-west, 'This is the city of Hadrian and not of Theseus'. Hadrian's philhellenic policies were continued by his immediate successors and Athens remained a centre for rich patrons of the arts. Herodes Atticus, for example, was one of the most prominent men in Athens. Living in his villa at Kifissia, then as now the suburban pleasance of Athenians, he commissioned the building of the Odeum, below the south-west corner of the acropolis, as a memorial to his wife Regilla who died in AD160. The work demanded so much material that the marble quarries of Mount Pentelicus were thought to have been exhausted. They survived, however, to provide enough marble in 1950–61 to refurbish and reseat the whole auditorium, which is now the chief venue of the annual Athens Festival. The name of Herodes Atticus is associated with other public buildings in Athens and also in Corinth, Delphi and Olympia.

Corinth

Athens was probably more prosperous under Hadrian and his contemporaries than at any period since its loss of independence, but it was not the greatest Graeco-Roman city of the south. This honour and distinction went to Corinth, though its site until 44BC lay desolate, the result of earlier destruction. In that year Julius Caesar refounded the city as a colony of veterans – Colonia Laus Julius Corinthienis – and its key position between the Saronic Gulf and the Gulf of Corinth again assured its commercial importance and prestige. Hadrian and other Roman notables added to Corinth's embellishments and by the end of the second century AD it was the showpiece of the Roman province and the first city in Greece.

Roman Corinth, however, was as much a city of pleasure as commerce and its inhabitants were notorious, in an age of licence, for their vices. The one thousand temple prostitutes, slave girls in the service of Aphrodite, undoubtedly provoked St Paul's reminder that 'bad company is the ruin of a good character' and he exhorted the Corinthians to 'return to a sober and upright life'. On his own admission Paul had come to Corinth 'in fear and in much trembling', though he spent eighteen months in the city as a missionary, at the same time plying his trade as a tentmaker in company with Aquila and Priscilla. His first epistle to the Corinthians provides a graphic picture of the internal troubles of the early church and of the frivolities, vices and perversions that made Corinth notorious.

Paul was obviously a disturbing element, especially among the purveyors of licentiousness, and on at least one occasion his preaching caused a riot in which he was attacked by a Greek mob. Neither were the Jews initially impressed, for they accused him, in the presence of the Roman governor, of corrupting the faith. However, Paul's two letters from Corinth to the local inhabitants, and those to the Thessalonians and the Romans, had the most profound influences in the development of Christianity. The Corinthians ultimately received what the pious would term their 'just rewards', perhaps not from the hand of the Almighty, but certainly from the attacks of barbarians and from a series of earthquakes which by the sixth century had devastated the city.

Delos

What Corinth stood for in terms of opulence, decadence and entertainment was matched by Delos' achievement as a cult and commercial centre, though this city, too, was not without its vices. Long before its involvement with Rome the small barren island which lacked all resources had gained both profit and glory from the worship of Apollo, who by tradition was born on the island. So sacred was Delos to the ancients that both the beginnings and ends of life were forbidden on its soil: women nearing their time and all who were near to death were ferried away from the island. Its great sanctuary, temples and other religious buildings, some devoted to Apollo's sister Artemis, attracted pilgrims from all over the ancient world and it was not long before Delos, aided by its central position in the Cyclades, began to flourish as a great emporium.

The city's trading values were given a tremendous boost when the Romans, to counterbalance the commercial powers of Rhodes, declared Delos a free port. By Strabo's time the great religious festivals had become major trade fairs and the city was embellished with monuments of all kinds as commercial houses and merchant syndicates from the eastern Mediterranean filled its coffers. Delos, however, also acquired a grim reputation as the great slave market of Greece with as many as 10,000 slaves changing hands on certain days.

The commercial decline of Delos was as swift as its rise to fame; trading alliances unfavourable to the city, sackings and piratical attacks quickly sapped its strength and Pausanias in his *Guide to Greece*, written cAD150, commented that 'were the temple guards withdrawn Delos would be uninhabited'. The modern temple guards are the archaeologists because Delos remains one of the richest ancient sites in Greece – a complete ruined city whose temples, theatres, streets, large villas and meaner quarters display every aspect of its ancient character. Uninhabited except for the excavators, the odd seasonal shepherd and the throng of summer tourists from neighbouring Myconos, Delos is a remarkable monument to Graeco-Roman civilisation.

ROME EAST AND WEST

The Roman peace was broken in AD175 by the Costoboci, a northern barbarian tribe who raided far into central Greece. Though defeated by the local militia, they were the vanguard of a series of raids from the north which proved to be of major importance in the subsequent history of the country. A more serious invasion was that of the Herulians, a Germano-Russian people who captured and pillaged Athens in AD267 before moving on to Corinth and other cities of the south. Ultimately, the Herulians were repulsed and Greece was spared from barbarian attacks for another century. But confidence in Roman arms and protection had been destroyed and as far as Athens was concerned the city retired behind a smaller circuit of walls which Valerian had built to enclose the northern slopes of the acropolis.

The mounting threat of barbarian raids throughout the Roman empire merely strengthened the long-held arguments for administrative reform and political reorganisation. Between AD285 and AD305 Diocletian, to facilitate internal control and protection from external threats, instituted a tetrarchy with a system of collegiate rule. A second Augustus, Maximian, was appointed for the defence of the west whose main strategic bases were Milan and Trier; while the east was defended from Sirmium on the Save coast and Nicomedia on the Marmora coast, the latter becoming Diocletian's capital. Each Augustus was aided by a Caesar in charge of the frontier regions, the idea being that the latter would understudy and replace the Augusti on retirement or death.

Diocletian had supposed that the tetrarchy system would largely put an end to usurpation by the ambitious. His scheme, however, all too logical in conception, was the cause of endless civil wars out of which emerged in AD308 the victorious Constantine the Great. After reuniting the empire, Constantine then readily accepted the practical necessity for its subdivision along the lines instituted by Diocletian. The great prefectures of Gallia and Italia formed the western empire, and Illyria and Oriens the eastern; the prefectures in turn consisted of several dioceses which were further subdivided into a large number of provinces. Under Constantine's successors the western and eastern empires were sometimes united but more generally they were separately ruled and what had started as an administrative partition between Latinised west and an essentially Hellenised east became a more fundamental separation.

The fates of the two empires were very different. The highly organised western frontier collapsed under the assaults of successive barbarian invasions, but the eastern empire, whose territories acquired the name Byzantine, survived into the thirteenth century and, in part, until 1453. 'Byzantine' is the expression of later generations, for the peoples of the empire considered themselves as Romans and their rulers as the successors and heirs to the Caesars. Yet though the beginnings of Byzantine history can be traced back to the Roman period, the highly civilised empire was more than a repository or inheritor of Graeco-Roman culture. With time it wandered further from the original characteristics of the Roman world, and the Greek language and culture and, in particular, the life of the Christian Church gained increasingly on its old Latin-pagan heritage. If Constantine the Great earned his epithet on the battlefield, he ensured its perpetuation by his defence and patronage of Christianity whose ideas were propagated by the universal Greek language. It has been suggested, in fact, that the common Greek heritage, primarily attributable to Alexander's conquests, was the chief factor not only in the empire's unity but also in its longevity. Though a constantly changing political expression, the Byzantine empire lasted longer than any other

in European history and from the fall of Rome in AD476 to that
of Constantinople in AD1453, it functioned as a military and
cultural bulwark for Europe against Asiatic aggression.

THE GREEK METROPOLIS

Constantine's other indelible mark on the history of the
Mediterranean world was the creation of the capital of the
Christian eastern empire at the old Greek colony of Byzantium
on the European shores of the Bosporus. The ancient Megarans
had fully appreciated the strategic and commercial advantages
of their prodigy and Byzantium played an important role in the
Graeco-Persian wars and during the conquests of Philip of
Macedon. Polybius recognised the colony's key position in
controlling 'the indispensable products of the Pontus' for
'without the consent of the inhabitants of Byzantium', he
continued, 'not a single vessel could enter or leave the Black
Sea'. Towards the end of the second century AD, Byzantium
received a heavy blow at the hand of the Romans for siding with
Pescennius Niger in his war against Septimus Severus.
Though sacked and almost completely destroyed in
retribution, its positional advantages demanded its rebuilding
and after AD203 Severus added the hippodrome, baths and
palaces, making Byzantium a Roman city of considerable
importance and distinction.

The reasons for Constantine's ultimate choice of Byzantium
as the site of his new capital is clothed in folklore and Christian
mythology, but with the insight of genius he had obviously
carefully appraised its political, cultural and economic
advantages. In the words of Myres (*Geographical History in Greek
Lands*) 'we have an example where a great statesman builded
better than he knew' for 'Constantinopolis' was destined to
become the largest urban concentration in medieval Europe
and the Near East. It was never a city state on the classical
Greek or Hellenistic patterns, but a metropolitan and
cosmopolitan capital of a large and centrally controlled empire.

Constantinople, almost impregnable to assaults by land and
sea, was both a natural and man-made city. The long inlet of

the Golden Horn, navigable for seven miles, formed with the Bosporus and the Sea of Marmora a readily defensible triangular peninsula. The rapid current that flows from the Black Sea to the Aegean, the harbour chains which in times of danger barred entrance to the Golden Horn, and the powerful sea walls combined to defend the city during many naval battles. The only successful assault occurred in 1204 when Venetian forces breached the walls of the Golden Horn, thus enabling the armies of the Fourth Crusade to take the city and parcel out its empire. It is significant that Constantinople was the last remnant of imperial territory to fall to the Latin feudatories at this time.

Very different were the city's defences on the landward side for here it was open to invasions across the Thracian lowlands, a weakness that had been remarked on by Polybius. Constantine's new walls stretched from the Golden Horn to the Sea of Marmora, roughly trebling the area occupied by the old Greek city. A further landward fortification was built by Theodosius II in AD413, partly to accommodate the city's rapid physical expansion, and extended in depth thirty-four years later. It was linked with a 19 mile circuit which also fortified the peninsula's seaward margins. Frequently restored during the Middle Ages, these walls remained impregnable for 1,000 years until they were breached by the Ottoman armies of Mehmet I on 29 May 1453.

Whereas local site factors explain Constantinople's function as a great fortress, geographical position was primarily responsible for its role as a centre of international commerce and communications. Unlike Rome, the city had a genuine economic viability, for at the junction of two inland seas and at the meeting-place of traditional overland routes, it acquired a natural wealth that came to be coveted by merchants and mercenaries throughout Europe and elsewhere. By the eleventh century the city's population was nearing the million mark and it seems to have presented a picture analogous to that of great modern cities, having all the complexities and defects concomitant with its metropolitan status, yet also preserving all the refinements of a remarkable urban society.

Constantinople became the Greek city *par excellence*, the 'Magna Graecia' of the Middle Ages and the 'Queen of Cities' which attracted world-wide scholars and travellers as well as merchants. In the face of the city's highly centralised and bureaucratic organisation, Greece itself was reduced to provincial status and, with the exception of Thessalonica, its cities had declined both in terms of population and in prestige. Though St Paul had preached the new religion at Athens, the city long remained proud of its famous shrines and centres of learning, resisting the Christian tendencies of the age. But in AD529 the Emperor Justinian closed its philosophy schools and turned its temples into churches. Athens had already been plundered of many art treasures, most of which had found their way to Constantinople, and the Parthenon was altered to become first the church of Aghia Sophia and subsequently that of the Virgin. Thus Constantinople, rather than Athens or any of the old cities, was increasingly accepted as the Greek capital, especially when the Christian church attacked former standards and attitudes. Such an aura has remained firmly fixed in the Greek mind and though a Turkish city since 1453, Constantinople's recovery as a Christian capital has constantly haunted the thinking of the Orthodox Church. Equally, dreams of the city returning to Greece has greatly coloured the country's politics, particularly during the nineteenth and early decades of this century. There are still Greeks who refuse to accept Constantinople as anything but irredentist Greek territory.

GREECE AND THE SLAVS

Much of the Greek mainland was Byzantium's least prosperous and most brutally exploited province. Military neglect of the Balkans in general meant that the land quickly fell victim to raiding and invasion, particularly by the Goths and the Huns who pillaged towns and countryside. Under their ambitious leader Alaric Balta, the Visigoths devastated Boeotia and Attica, sacking Eleusis and Piraeus though sparing Athens in return for heavy contributions. According to the historian

Zosimus, Alaric was induced to save the city by the apparition of the goddess Athena pleading for her citizens!

These raids were but preludes to far greater population movements from beyond the Danube and one of the most important factors in the history of Greece from the sixth to the twelfth centuries was the complete breakdown of Byzantium's northern frontier, leading to both raids and settlements by Bulgars, Avars and Slavs. Attacks by the Slavs assumed massive proportions during the reign of Justinian I (527–565) who inaugurated an ambitious, but belated, defence programme which included a wall across the isthmus at Corinth supported by a series of fortresses and a large number of bastions. After AD580, a combined force of Avars and Slavs, estimated at 10,000, poured into northern Greece. Thessalonica withstood assault on three occasions but by 623 the raids had reached the Aegean and Crete.

Concurrently with the military attacks on Byzantine cities a more peaceful occupation of the Greek mainland was underway as Slav raiding gradually changed to land settlement. The Slavs seemed to have developed few political institutions and their status in Greece is succinctly defined in the *Chronicle of Monemvasia* which describes them as being 'subject neither to the emperor of the Romans, nor to anyone else'. So widespread had their settlements become, however, that by the eighth century the southern Balkans, including the Greek mainland was known as 'Sclavinia', a term of key importance in the medieval and subsequent history of Greece.

Much heated argument has centred on the Slav element in the Greek population and the controversy entered an acute stage in the early decades of the nineteenth century when Fallermayer propounded the view that the Slav, and later Albanian, immigrants eclipsed the old Greek stock. The 'modern' Greeks, he maintained, had 'not a single drop of Greek blood in their veins'. Such a theory became a strong political weapon in the Eastern Question and was challenged both by diplomats and by the learned world. Many philhellenes and neo-classicists, for example, interested in the struggle for Greek independence (see Chapter 6) laid great stress on the continuity and illustrious ancestry of the Greeks. Fallermayer's thesis is now largely discredited though it is accepted that the Slavs made a considerable contribution to the peopling of medieval Greece as the numerous Slav place names testify. Byzantium was indeed forced to implement an extensive policy of political and cultural assimilation in which the main tenets of Greek Byzantine life – language and the Orthodox religion – naturally played active and, it appears, successful roles.

THESSALONICA

One of the main bulwarks against Slav and other incursions was the city of Thessalonica which, unlike the Byzantine Greek cities of the south, had materially prospered from the empire's early days. Its geographical position and consequent commercial and strategic advantages made it a major international market and both in size and in prestige it became Byzantium's second city. Though proving less impregnable than Constantinople, Thessalonica's massive fortifications were able to withstand successive attacks from Goths, Avars, Bulgars, Slavs and Saracen corsairs. Providing an impressive example of Byzantine and earlier military architecture, the ramparts which today form a lofty and theatrical skyline at the summit of the city are the remains of a separately walled and towered citadel whose course perpetuates the early Hellenistic enceinte. It was formerly linked with the defences of the lower city but here there are few military remains, the exception being the massive White Tower, the principal feature of the modern city's esplanade.

The Byzantine court frequently resided at Thessalonica and the city enjoyed great privileges, including its own measure of autonomy with an elected senate, administrative officials and civil guard. The city even sent envoys abroad to discuss and foster commercial relationships which were reflected in its great annual fair dedicated to St Demetrios, the patron saint, and held at the time of his feast. The twelfth-century author of the satirical *Timarion* graphically describes the variety of goods and

(*above*) The Little Metropolis, Athens, is an almost perfect example of a small Byzantine church dating from the twelfth century. Though now dominated by the new cathedral and modern city blocks the proportions of the Metropolis were compatible with the modest buildings in Athens prior to the city's selection as capital in the nineteenth century;* (*below*) the compact village of Lindos on the island of Rhodes. Though now an agricultural and tourist village it traces its history back to classical times and was one of the fortress centres of the Knights of St John

Throughout this century Athens has developed rapidly along
western lines and has spread beyond the formerly isolated hills of
the Attic Plain. Like most large conurbations it suffers from the
full range of planning problems and its urban reorganisation is
constantly under discussion

The Street of the Knights, reconstructed during the Italian occupation of Rhodes, represents one of the most remarkable survivals of a late medieval thoroughfare in Europe. Its tidiness, however, unusual in Greek towns, slightly detracts from the full spirit and feeling of the Middle Ages

peoples which annually met on the banks of the Vardar outside the city walls. Merchants were attracted from the
Mediterranean lands, the Near East and from as far away as
France and Flanders and, as in Constantinople, the Venetians
and other Italian trading states acquired their own quarters in
the city. Thessalonica's main ethnic group was the Jews, but it
was not until the sixteenth century, following their expulsion
from Spain and southern Germany, that they constituted the
major part of the population.

Thessalonica's commercial strength and imperial prestige
naturally favoured artistic and intellectual development. As
scholars from many countries popularised its schools and
colleges it became a sort of 'Athens' of medieval Hellenism
where intellectual activity and theological discussion combined
to make it one of the spiritual centres of Byzantium. Thus its
most impressive buildings were Christian churches and 365 are
said to have existed in the medieval town. Today only 20 (9 in
their original form) have survived conquest, conversion (and re-
conversion) to other faiths, and fire. Throughout its history the
city has been particularly prone to fires. One of the most
devastating occurred on 5 August 1917 and made 50,000 people
homeless and destroyed many churches and public buildings.
Those churches that survive include the rotunda of St George,
originally a Roman building, the basilica of St Demetrios and
the churches of St Sophia, St Paraskevi, St Catherine and the
Holy Apostles. Through their architecture and mosaic
decoration it is possible to trace the whole process of Byzantine
ecclesiastical development from the fourth to the fourteenth
centuries. Yet Thessalonica illustrates continuity in other
ways. The city's great boast and pride is that it has always been
a Greek city, founded in Hellenistic times, and never a mere
satellite or shadow of Constantinople or, today, of Athens. In
history it was often in the foreground of Greek thought,
pioneering many national reforms. In contemporary Greece
the annual Thessalonica trade fair, one of the largest in Eastern
Europe and the Mediterranean, perpetuates the city's role as a
centre of international commerce while on the intellectual level
its university continues the progressive traditions of the past.

5

The Banners of Religion

The large number of Frankish castles and fortified towers that punctuate the landscape of mainland Greece and the islands testify to the impact and arguable success of the Fourth Crusade of 1204 when the Greek lands lost their unity and their history again became the story, not of one, but of many separate states. Setting out with the laudable intention of rescuing the Holy Sepulchre in Jerusalem from Moslem hands, the Crusade had turned aside to the easier and more lucrative task of seizing the Byzantine empire. Venice, under its wily Doge Dandolo, was entirely responsible for this for the Republic had long cast covetous eyes on the rich Byzantine cities and was intent on displacing all western merchants, particularly its traditional rivals, the Genoese, from the Greek markets.

Venice was the Crusade's chief financier and in return for providing the indispensable naval transports, promising also to supply the armies for one year, Dandolo successfully diverted the Crusaders to an attack first on the Adriatic port of Zara, which had rebelled against Venetian authority, and then on Constantinople. Thus, instead of attacking the Infidel, the Soldiers of the Cross basely made war on their fellow Christians, taking Constantinople after a long siege and dividing its spoils and its empire among themselves. With commercial greed at its heart the Fourth Crusade earned for itself the title of the 'greatest commercial coup of all times'.

Constantinople, its palaces, churches, villas and libraries, witnessed one of the greatest sackings in history. Geoffrey Villehardouin, the Crusade's historian, wrote that it was impossible to count the gold, silver, jewels, silks and furs that fell into western hands. Of the portable relics of nine centuries of Byzantine history that now survive a great number are still

Greece in the early thirteenth century

to be seen in triumphant Venice, though many also ended up in Germany. Not content with riches, the Crusaders proceeded to ridicule the Greek faith by placing a prostitute on the throne of St Sophia and turning Orthodox masses into drunken orgies. In the Thessalonican churches they howled like dogs to mock the chants of the Greek priests and used the 'miraculous' oil which oozed from the tomb of St Demetrios to polish their boots. Though the Turks, 300 years later, committed many atrocities, even exhuming the body of the saint and hacking the skeleton to pieces, they generally treated the Orthodox Church with greater respect, hence the resounding cry of the last three centuries of Byzantine history: 'Better the Turks than the Latins!'

THE LATIN STATES

Once in possession of Constantinople, avarice and ambition inevitably involved the Crusaders in disputes over the imperial throne. These were partly resolved when Count Baldwin of Flanders was proclaimed the first Latin Emperor of Constantinople and ruled over a restricted territory lying athwart the Sea of Marmora. In Greece proper a number of Latin states were established in what had been Byzantine imperial territory though their boundaries, rulers and allegiances were often ephemeral. Boniface de Montferrat, Commander-in-Chief of the Crusader forces, gained the prized Kingdom of Thessalonica (1204–24) which included Macedonia, Thessaly and much of central Greece. To the south the Lordship or Duchy of Athens (1204–1456) passed to Othon de la Roche, a Burgundian noble and an associate of Boniface, and the Peloponnesus fell to the Villehardouin family as the Principality of Achaia or the Morea (1204–1432). Numerous lesser margraviates, counties and baronies were dependent on these major states for, in true feudal fashion, grants of land were given by the ruling overlords as a reward for service and as a well-tried policy of colonisation. Achaia, for example, was partitioned into twelve baronies each with their castle strongholds and the Kingdom of Thessalonica included the fief of Larisa, ruled by a Lombard noble, a Rhenish county based on Valestino and the Thermopylae area which passed to the Pallavincini family from near Parma.

It was Venice, however, both from the strategic and commercial points of view, that secured the choicest of the Greek lands, acquiring control of three-quarters of Constantinople, most of the Aegean and Ionian islands, Crete, Euboea and several important points in the Peloponnesus, including the fortresses of Modon (Methone) and Cronon which guarded the sea route to the east. Ultimately, other territories came under the powerful banner of the Lion of St Mark and the Venetian sea-state developed as a series of commercial stepping-stones and strategic positions strung along the major medieval trade routes of the eastern Mediterranean. 'Never', we are told, 'was there a state so dependent on the sea.'

Realising the practical difficulties of administrating discontinuous territories the Venetians, like the feudal lords of the mainland, awarded land grants and dependencies to their own nobles in return for trading privileges in the newly created fiefdoms. The occupation of the Aegean islands, allotted to Venice in 1204, was left to private citizens and Marco Sanudo, a buccaneering nephew of the Doge, set out with other adventuring companions to win for themselves a principality. After taking Naxos the reduction of eleven other islands followed, including the neighbouring Paros and Antiparos, Ios, Amorges, Cynthnos, Siphnos and Melos. Other Venetian nobles acquired the surrounding islands as fiefs, paying homage to Sanudo as Duke of Naxos, though the combined island principality stretching from the Northern Sporades (Skyros, Skopelos and Skiathos) to the volcanic Thera or Santorini, became known as the Duchy of the Archipelago. Based on a prosperous agriculture and sea trade the Duchy, under a number of dynasties, was the most durable of the Latin states, lasting from 1207 until the Turkish raids of 1566, though the island of Tinos resisted until 1718.

The Venetians operated a similar colonising and control policy in the Ionian islands of Zante, Cefalonia and Ithaca which came to be governed by Matthew Orosini as the County Palatine of Cefalonia. But Paxos and Corfu, the latter subsequently becoming one of Venice's prize maritime possessions, remained in the hands of Leone Vetrano, an infamous Genoese pirate. In 1206 a large Venetian fleet commanded by Dandolo's son took Corfu which, a year later, was transferred to the care of ten Venetian noblemen. The initial occupation was of short duration but in 1387 the Republic repossessed the island commencing a period of unbroken rule which lasted 410 years. Up to 1797, when it was taken by the French, Corfu grew rich as a centre of east-west trade and when Greece fell to the Ottoman Turks it became the militant symbol of the Christian west, acting as a significant boundary stone in the history of the Moslem advance.

The Genoese, ever eager to break Venetian trading monopoly in the eastern Mediterranean, had also initially installed themselves on Crete where, with the aid of the islanders, they resisted Venetian intervention. In 1210 they were driven out and the appointment of Jacopo Tiepolo as first governor began Crete's long occupation by the Venetians. Naming the island and its capital 'Candia' they immediately began its fortification and organisation, dividing the lands into six sections corresponding it is said to the six quarters of Venice, which were then thrown open to Venetian colonisers and entrepreneurs. To develop the city it was enacted that the Venetian nobility and the local Greek aristocracy must build houses in it and reside there for part of the year. Candia (modern Iraklion) was destined to become one of the leading seaports of the eastern Mediterranean and its impressive, and almost indestructible, walls, bastions and fortifications (dating from the fourteenth to the seventeenth centuries) were to make its name synonymous with gallant resistance. The Venetians also rebuilt and fortified Canea which briefly enjoyed the reputation of being 'the Venice of the East', and other thriving Venetian towns included Rethymnon, Sitia and Kastelli, all, in spite of considerable damage, still bearing the distinctive imprint of the Venetian period.

Unlike that of the Ionian islands, however, the Venetian occupation of Crete was oppressive and attempts to impose their own way of life on the islanders were met with many bloody revolts in which Italian colonists joined the Cretans. Only towards the end of the Republic's rule, when Turkish pressure necessitated local support, was the regime relaxed and the former heavy and unjust exactions reduced.

CHURCH, CASTLE AND COURT

For the Venetians, as for the majority of the western feudatories, Greece was little more than a land of opportunity and adventure in which fortunes could be made, possibly to pay off debts, even crimes, incurred at home. Mostly they were birds of passage though the passage could be delayed a century or so, even longer in the case of the Venetians in Corfu, Crete and Euboea. Many came solely to amuse themselves in medieval pageantry, but the life of chivalry they tried to introduce was of minor appeal to the Greeks. The *Chronicle of*

Monemvasia, versions of which occur in a variety of European languages, describes the life of Frankish society which operated from a number of fortresses in an otherwise foreign land. It provides a vivid picture of the strange mixture of nationalities and of social and political institutions. There was little fraternisation between rulers and subject peoples and, with few exceptions, hardly any intermarriage. That the writer was a true Frank is obvious from the *Chronicle*'s Catholic and western sympathies.

The Franks took over the existing Greek ecclesiastical organisation and though the inferior clergy were allowed to remain, provided they acknowledged the primacy of the Pope, the orthodox archbishops and bishops were replaced by those of the Latin faith. Attempts to unite the churches of Rome and Constantinople proved fruitless and there were comparatively few converts to Catholicism except in the Ionian islands and the Cyclades where Latin rule remained longest; today, for example, Tinos and Syros, and to a lesser degree Naxos, Corfu and some other islands retain substantial Catholic populations. By the fourteenth century, however, the Orthodox clergy were returning to their sees and the Greeks found in them allies and leaders against foreign rule – culturally and politically. The memory of Constantinople's sacking and the degradation of Orthodoxy remained firmly embedded in the minds of the Greeks and distrust of, and hostility to, the Franks, was understandably strong among the monks and clergy. What was happening concerning religion was also echoed in language for both peasants and church and other officials clung dutifully to the Greek tongue and when, in 1259, Godfrey de Brieres exclaimed 'we speak one tongue' it was a reference to the Frankish knights speaking the Greek vernacular.

The Franks, therefore, remained largely as strangers among the native population, to whom the presence of knights in shining armour engaged in hunting, jousting, feasting and even troubadouring, must have appeared more than a little odd. Compared to that of the Greek countryside, life in the Frankish palace-fortresses was often magnificently developed and the castle of Chlemousti on the west coast of the Peloponnesus near

Cyllene is one of the most impressive monuments to Frankish rule in Greece. Built in 1220–3 by Geoffrey I Villehardouin, who called it Clairmont, its keep and inner bailey perched on a hill, with its outer bailey protecting the most exposed slope is typical of the Frankish fortresses built to maintain a somewhat precarious hold over a numerically superior subject peoples. At Chlemousti and at nearby Gastouni and Andravida, Godfrey II Villehardouin indulged his flamboyance by demanding the constant attendance of eighty knights with golden spurs and during the rule of William II Villehardouin the same court housed 800 of the flower of western European chivalry. The Peloponnesus was a favoured training ground for knightly practice and in 1305 an international tournament was held at Corinth between twelve great champions of the west and the Greek-based chivalry. In particular, William's court attracted the younger generation who, it is reported, valued physical beauty as highly as valour yet, according to Froissart, it was the fifteenth-century court of Cefalonia that was the 'second fairyland' in terms of knightly demands!

The most notable among the Greek states for pageantry, splendour and luxury was the Duchy of Athens. During the reign of Guy II its courts at Athens and Thebes won the admiration even of visitors familiar with the great assemblies of western Europe and the excellent French spoken at Athens was remarked on. The Burgundian princes were mild and pacific rulers who encouraged agriculture, trade and manufacturing. The traditional silk industry based at Thebes was of international reputation and the earner of great profits: Theban silks had been worn by both Byzantine emperors and popes. But the Duchy's period of brilliance was not destined to last for long and in Greece the wisdom and style of its rulers were soon forgotten. In western Europe, however, probably out of nostalgia, their memory lingered and it was Frankish Athens and a Frankish duke, albeit named Theseus, whose court Shakespeare chose as the background of his *A Midsummer Night's Dream*. Yet it is perhaps Demetrius in that play who summarises the legacy of the medieval Duchy and of Frankish Greece as a whole:

> These things seem small and indistinguishable, like far-off
> mountains turned into clouds

Many historians have agreed, and regard the Latin rule in
Greece as a historical accident irrelevent to the ultimate destiny
of its people.

The Knights of St John

No account of medieval chivalry in Greece would be complete
without reference to the Knights of the Order of St John of
Jerusalem who were established on Rhodes and other
Dodecanese islands from 1309 to 1522. The Order, like the
Templars and the Teutonic Order, was the direct product of
the Crusades, and originated as a hospice, founded by Amalfi
merchants whose purpose was the lodging and succouring of
Christian pilgrims on their way to the Holy Land. Following
the success of the First Crusade, however, the knights
transformed themselves into a military body, extending their
protective role, though still continuing with their nursing and
sheltering duties. Having been forced out of Palestine following
the loss of their possessions to the Arabs at Acre and Krak de
Chevaliers, they settled briefly in Cyprus. Their possession of
Rhodes, confirmed by Pope Clement V, gave them for the first
time full territorial sovereignty and they were quick to
recognise the island as a suitable location for a permanent base
from which to contest the Moslem advance. Defence of the
church against the Moslem 'infidel' now became the Order's
prime objective, though its members were still required to make
three fundamental vows of chastity, obedience and poverty.

On their arrival in Rhodes the Order had settled into three
classes: the knights militant, recruited only from noble
families; the serving brothers or fighting squires who made up a
corps of nurses and assistants and followed the knights into
battle; and the chaplains and almoners who attended to
religious matters. To enter the Order as a prospective knight, a
youth had to prove himself to be of unblemished noble and
Catholic parentage and an exhaustive inquiry was conducted
into each postulant's eligibility. Nobles were admitted at the

age of fourteen and enjoyed the privileges of residing in the fortress and wearing the full dress of the Order. The admission of full privilege to arms, however, could not be confirmed before the age of eighteen. The youthfulness of the knights was remarkable and so great were the dangers and hardships of their chosen life, hardly one knight in twenty lived to reach the age of fifty. Yet a great deal of romantic sentiment is conjured up by the knights and it should be stressed that the Order quickly became aggressively military and Rhodes developed into a naval power of aristocratic corsairs. They laudably maintained their hospital, though for their own kind, and it was knightly patients and no one else who ate from the famous silver plates.

The knights were grouped, according to their country of origin into *langues* or *tongues* – Provence, Auvergne, France, Italy, Spain, Germany and England. Each *tongue* had its own headquarters known as an inn, which was under the command of a bailiff. Collectively the bailiffs constituted the Chapter of the Order, presided over by an elected Grand Master of which a total of nineteen served on Rhodes. Their inscriptions and escutcheons adorn the formidable ramparts, towers, bastions, defended gateways and barbicans which are magnificent examples of fourteenth– to sixteenth–century military architecture. Largely due to the restoration work of the Italians, who occupied Rhodes and the Dodecanese from 1912 to 1943, these fortifications and much of the old town of the knights remain intact. Within the defences the old Collachium quarter, formerly separated from the Bourg or merchant's town by an internal wall, contains the hospital, the inns of the *tongues*, some of the administrative buildings of the holy religion and the palace-fortress of the Grand Masters. Its discreetly restored principal street, popularly called the 'Street of the Knights', represents one of the most remarkable survivals of a late medieval thoroughfare in Europe, though its tidiness, usual in Greek towns, slightly detracts from the full spirit and feeling of the Middle Ages.

The knights had other defences on Rhodes, including their great fortress on the acropolis at Lindos, and the islands of

Alimnia, Tilos, Nisiros, Kalimnos, Leros and Kos, as well as Budrum on the Anatolian coast, were all heavily protected against Asiatic aggression. Kos (famous in antiquity as the birthplace of Hippocrates and as one of the main medical centres of Asclepios), was occupied by the knights from 1315 until, like Rhodes, it fell to the Ottomans in 1522. The impressive fortress still guards its harbour against the entry of large ships, though unfortunately much of the old town was destroyed in the disastrous earthquake on 23 April 1933. Yet earthquakes in Greece tend to bring advantages to the archaeologists for the ruined town, again under Italian direction was excavated between 1935 and 1943 revealing extensive classical Roman remains. The new Kos was developed on the site of the old Turkish quarter and beyond it.

In this brief outline of the Knights of St John with its references to conquest by the Ottoman Turks, Greek history has been outstepped. The Frankish and Byzantine ages were indeed complex and before Greece fell to the Turks Byzantium experienced a political and cultural revival which was the culmination of a steady progress since 1204.

BYZANTIUM RENASCENT

Contemporary with the fluctuating fortunes of the Latin states three Greek monarchies were founded on the ruins of the former Byzantine empire. Of these, the one centred on Trebizond on the Black Sea had little major impact on Greek development, but in western Asia Minor and in Epirus representatives of the old Byzantine emperors were instrumental in winning back something of the empire's former glory. The Latin rulers of Constantinople had little control over the Asia Minor territories, and from the rich city of Nicaea (modern Iznik) close to the Marmora coast, Theodore Lascaris, the son-in-law of a former Byzantine emperor, established a court which soon matured as the centre of a small, but reviving Greek empire. Lascaris had the strong support of the Greek clergy who, recognising him as the lawful and legitimate ruler, urged him to retake Constantinople. The greater part of the Kingdom of Thessalonica was annexed in 1246 by a successor, John Vatatzes, but it was under the rule of the noble family of Palaeologos that the Empire of Nicaea rapidly advanced in political power. Constantinople and its Latin empire, after a short life of only fifty-seven years, fell to the Nicaean Greeks in 1261. Its last ruler, also named Baldwin, fled to the west where the empty title of 'Latin Emperor' continued until the death of the last holder in 1383.

Possession of Thessalonica was the recognised first goal of every usurper to the imperial throne and prior to its inclusion within Nicaea it was occupied by Michael Angelus Comnenus as part of the Despotate of Epirus (1204–1336). Michael, a representative of the imperial family and contender to the throne, had seized the difficult country of Epirus and, out of an initial resistance movement against Latin encroachment, forged a powerful kingdom extending from Durazzo in the north to Naupaktos on the Gulf of Corinth in the south. Like its rival Nicaea, the Despotate became a refuge for Greek patriotism and its courts at Arta and Ioannina flourished as important cultural centres, the latter receiving refugees from both Constantinople and the Peloponnesus. Arta retains many reminders of its period of medieval brilliance including the late Byzantine-style church of Panaghia Parigoritissa (now a museum) built by Michael and his consort Anna. The churches of Saints Basil, Theodora, Dimitrios and Nicholas, today beautifully restored, are other fine examples of Byzantine ecclesiastical architecture, as are the nearby monasteries of Vlachernae and Kato Panaghia.

Ultimately, the Despotate of Epirus proved no match for the expansionist policies of the Byzantine Palaeologi who had acquired important territorial gains in the Peloponnesus. The involvement of William II Villehardouin in the disputes between Epirus and Constantinople led to his capture by Michael III Palaeologos and freedom was only restored in return for the Frankish fortresses of Monemvasia, Maina and Mistra, these three becoming the important southern bases from which, by 1432, the whole of the Peloponnesus was restored to Byzantine rule.

Mistra, situated in the foothills of the Taygetus mountains five kilometres west of Sparta, was reported as being William's favourite stronghold. It was built to dominate the Slav settlements of the Eurotas valley and the hill tribes of the Taygetus; but from this site earlier in history the Spartans had thrown their deformed or weak children to their death. The installation of a Byzantine despot at Mistra, either a son or brother of the emperor (often his heir presumptive), led to its rapid growth as one of the most important political and cultural centres of renascent Byzantium, surviving the fall of Constantinople to the Turks by seven years. Theologians, philosophers, architects and artists flooded to Mistra and collectively they developed a high level of originality in both intellectual and artistic achievement. Such originality was the product of Mistra's close ties with Constantinople on the one hand and of its provincial Greek location on the other. Many maintain that Mistra possessed much of the spirit of ancient Greece and the teachings of its thinkers and artists became much valued in Renaissance Italy. It retained its creative spirit to the end and at its fall in 1460 graphic accounts are given of poets, scholars, painters and philosophers stubbornly defending its walls against the onslaughts of the Ottoman Turks.

Under the Ottomans, but particularly under its brief period of Venetian rule (1687–1715), Mistra remained a populous and rich city whose main industry was silk worm culture. But in 1770 an abortive revolt led to its destruction by the Sultan's Albanian forces. Some semblance of transient life continued amongst its ruins until 1952 when the last families were evacuated by the Greek Archaeological Society. Today Mistra is a deserted city but the ancient stones of its ramparts and houses, its churches, monasteries and palaces, all clinging to the side of its rocky hill, evoke an amazing picture of medieval Greece and provide a rich haven for the student of Byzantine civilisation.

VLACHS, ALBANIANS AND JEWS

As if to complicate further its already rich ethnic fabric a number of other peoples emerge in the history of Greece during the Middle Ages. Perhaps the most colourful yet problematic in terms of origins are the Koustovlachs who appear in the Byzantine sources of the eleventh and twelfth centuries in much the same guise as their modern descendents. Although they have their own established villages in the Pindus ranges where they live by pastoralism and forestry the Vlachs are, by tradition, transhumant herders who move with their flocks of sheep, goats and often horses between the summer pastures in the mountains and the winter settlements in the Thessalian plains and elsewhere. The picturesque town of Metsovon high in the mountainous fastness of the Pindus has a considerable Vlach population and here, and in other communities, both men and women wear their traditional dress. For the former it consists of a blue serge tunic, belted at the waist, long white woollen stockings and a little round black cap, and for the latter a low-waisted red dress bordered with black and with loose sleeves, very wide at the cuffs. These costumes are particularly common in the town of Trikkala whose population during the winter months is significantly increased by the influx of Vlachs driven out from the mountains by inclement weather. They bring with them woollen rugs and locally embroidered textiles whose traditional character has changed little through the centuries. The Byzantines knew them for their textiles, chiefly the homespun coats which were much prized by the poorer classes of Constantinople and Thessalonica.

Vlach origins are obscure though they claim, with some degree of probability, to descend from Roman colonists in the Danube basin. Formerly they were far more numerous than today, occupying the larger part of western Macedonia and Thessaly and establishing in the twelfth century a Bulgaro-Vlach state which survived until the coming of the Turk. Around 1170, the Jewish traveller Benjamen of Tudela referred to the mountainous region of Thessaly as Wallachia and its inhabitants he called Vlachi. 'They are as nimble as deer', he stated, 'and descend from the mountains into the plains of Greece committing robberies and taking booty. Nobody ventures to make war on them, nor can any king bring them to submission.' This fierce independence was based on their sense of being different for Vlach or Wallach, meaning 'stranger', was applied to them by their neighbours; they referred to themselves as Aromani (Romans), their language in fact being a dialect of Romanian with the expected admixture of Greek, Slav, Turkish and Albanian words, all fully or partly Hellenised. Their probable Romanian origin played a significant part in Balkan politics during the early years of this century, for Romania claimed them and even set up a system of Vlach education (conducted in Romanian) centred on Florina and Thessalonica. The Vlachs and their descendants, however, have played important roles in Greek national life and it is significant that one of the forerunners of Greek independence was a Vlach, Constantine Rhidas, from Valestino near the Thessalian port of Volos.

Next to the Slavs the Albanians form the most important group of settlers that have affected the ethnic composition of the Greeks. Descendants of Illyrian tribes, they moved southwards into Greece during the fourteenth century spreading into Acarnania, Aeotolia and Thessaly where their raiding gradually passed into settlement. Many, however, were induced or invited to the Byzantine and Latin states to fight as mercenaries or to settle as colonists along open frontiers. Those who came to Venetian controlled Euboea, for example, were granted land and tax exemptions provided they brought and kept horses for the defence of the island. Others were invited to the Peloponnesus, particularly to Mistra, and many settled in Boeotia and Attica where their descendants still speak an Albanian dialect along with their Greek. From time to time ill-treatment by local officials led to Albanian uprisings though cultural assimilation was quick, especially in the towns, and the Albanians became ardent Greek patriots in the War of Independence. Many who settled on the Argo-Saronic islands of Poros, Hydra and Spetses won fame and fortune as nineteenth-century merchant-corsairs.

Unlike the Vlachs and Albanians the Jews of Greece were urban dwellers who, in characteristic manner, played a major role in commercial life. As early as 1170 Benjamen of Tudela found flourishing colonies at Thebes, Thessalonica, Corinth and Chalkis and there were smaller communities elsewhere. At Thebes he describes them as the 'most eminent manufacturers of silk and purple cloth', and the city's Jewish scholars were second only to those of Constantinople. The Jews were particularly attracted by the commercial advantages of the Venetian colonies, though they paid heavily for their privileges often becoming the scapegoats for higher taxation exacted to meet strategic and economic expediences. An exception was their protected position on Corfu, but even here a series of injunctions bidding the Corfiotes to treat them well would seem to suggest that this protection was seldom efficacious against traditional prejudices. The real influx of Jews into Greece came with their expulsion from Spain and Portugal in 1492 and from Naples, Apulia and Calabria half a century later. In 1665 there were some 500 Jewish houses in Corfu though the main urban attractions were Constantinople and Thessalonica, in Turkish hands by this time and, according to Giovanni Botero, collectively housing 160,000 Jews. They prospered under the Turks and Thessalonica, whose commercial life was greatly stimulated, came to be regarded as a Jewish city with its own schools, hospitals and charitable institutions.

THE OTTOMAN ADVANCE

The Ottoman conquest of Greece was favoured by circumstances and long before the fall of Constantinople in 1453 the Turks were in control of almost all of mainland Greece, and possession of the majority of the Aegean islands soon followed. The political and social fragmentation of Greece (in reality a jigsaw puzzle of disunited princedoms), coupled with the religious conflict between Catholicism and Orthodoxy, made it in the words of Fernand Braudel 'a mere house of cards' capable of offering little more than token resistance. The Turks had initially arrived from Asia Minor at the request of the Byzantine emperor to assist in the struggle against the Serbs, but having defeated them they refused to return, undertaking instead a long and successful military campaign in Thrace. Adrianople (modern Edirne) became their capital and the base from which the conquest of south-east Europe began. The chronology of the Turkish advance is confusing, but during the next century the Greek states fell in succession, and victory was particularly rapid in the extensive plains of northern and central Greece where the Turks settled their own people and heavily overlaid these regions with their own civilisation. Though the city of Thessalonica probably resisted until 1430 Macedonia was occupied by 1380 and Thessaly annexed in 1393. The mountainous west and peninsular south proved more difficult and control was more often apparent than real; Ioannina, however, fell in 1430 and by 1460 the Duchy of Athens was occupied.

The Turkish conquest of the Peloponnesus was assisted by the actions of two of its rival rulers, Demetrios Palaeologus at Mistra and his brother Thomas at Patras, who in 1453 simultaneously appealed to the Turks for help against Albanian incursions. The Turkish general Turakhan, eager to assist, completed his task by conquering the brothers and in 1458 Mehmet II ordered the invasion of the Peloponnesus under the leadership of Turakhan's son, Omar. By 1461, apart from the Venetian-held coastal points, it was completed. Venice, in fact, became the main challenger to the Ottoman advance and the field of conquest shifted from mainland Greece to the Aegean and surrounding seas in which some of the most famous battles and sieges in medieval history were enacted. Constantly exhausted by the Moslem threat, the Venetian 'limes' were by the sixteenth century reduced to a string of archaic forts which acted more as impediments than deterrents to Turkish progress. The Republic's major ally, however, was Rhodes where in 1480 the Knights of St John had successfully defended their possessions against a powerful Turkish force despatched by Mohammed the Conqueror, the new ruler of Constantinople.

The fall of Rhodes was merely delayed for on 22 December

1522 Sultan Suleiman II (the Magnificent) mounted his great siege which lasted 177 days. Three hundred ships and over 100,000 men are said to have made up the Ottoman force, and although these figures may be suspect, there is no doubt that the besiegers possessed an overwhelming majority. The knights, it seems, mustered 650 with the addition of 6,000 Rhodians and a contingent of around 700 extras made up of Venetians, Genoese and Cretans. Rhodes put up tremendous resistance and Suleiman, greatly discouraged by his losses, was about to lift the siege when the knights were betrayed by one of their own number. Informed of their depleted resources, Suleiman continued the onslaught until the city was surrendered by Grand Master Villiers de l'Isle Adam. Guaranteed their lives the knights, escorted by 4,000 inhabitants, withdrew to Viterbo and Civitavecchia, eventually establishing themselves in Malta. This was under a grant of Charles V of Spain who had remarked on hearing the story of the great siege that 'Nothing in the world was ever so well lost as was Rhodes'.

With the knights dispersed and Chios and the Duchy of the Archipelago (with the exception of Tinos) falling in 1566, the Turks were in almost complete control of the Aegean. They regarded Crete, therefore, as one of the last barriers to the west and certainly, following the fall of Constantinople, the island became one of the last outposts of Orthodox Greek culture where scholars and artists, fleeing from the mainland, developed a distinctive style in which Greek and Venetian traditions were blended. This late renaissance of Byzantine art resulted in the fine fresco paintings of many Cretan churches. Notable icon painters included Tzanfournares, Klotsas, Dhamaskinos and the legendary Domenico Theotokopoulos (El Greco) whose major works were accomplished in Venice and Spain. Though the literary products of this period are not generally known outside Greece they too were influential and the epic poem *Erotocritos* by Vincenzo Cornaros played a major role in the moulding of modern Greek literature. In addition to the works of art and literature, numerous public buildings were erected in the Cretan cities; docks, harbours and wharves were constructed and, most significantly, fortifications were extended and strengthened.

In 1645 the Turks mounted a fleet which took Canea, and Rethymnon fell in the following year. Candia, however, became the last Venetian resistance point in the Aegean and its epic siege beginning in 1648 lasted for more than twenty years, in which 30,000 Venetians and allies are said to have been lost and 118,000 Turks. During its last two years, with the eyes of western Europe upon it, Candia was defended by Francesco Morosini, but it finally surrendered and the Turks allowed the defenders to leave with honour. Some settled in the southern Peloponnesus, others moved to Corsica (where a variation of the Cretan dialect was reported as surviving until quite recently) and others to the Venetian Ionian islands, the only part of Greece to escape Ottoman domination.

IN THE DIVAN

History has not always judged the Turkish occupation of Greece with detachment. One point immediately in its favour is the period of stable political conditions it brought, a *pax turkica*, where the Greek lands, divided among so many sovereignties since 1204, once more found some form of unity in a foreign rule centred on Constantinople. The Turks, it is true, left few visible traces on Greece, and the disabilities they imposed were often severe, yet it would be unfair to condemn the Turkish period as one of unmitigated disaster. The new order meant that the Greek peoples gradually found, or were given, their place in the empire and by collaborating with (at least initially), rather than openly resisting the new rulers, some segments of the population maintained or acquired a degree of prosperity. Postel, Belon and Villamont – French travellers of the sixteenth century – wrote favourably about the character of the Turks and their good conduct towards the Greeks, and others admired the order and discipline prevailing throughout the empire and particularly in the army which maintained the peace. Such views, of course, are subjective, but it is fair to say that the most detailed accounts of Turkish Greece stem from

visitors during the nineteenth century, a time when the
Ottoman empire was rapidly disintegrating and the symptoms
of the 'sick old man of Europe' appeared in the guises of
inefficiency, corruption and violence. The view of the enslaved
Greek exposed to humiliation, dishonour and slaughter by the
hands of violent and tyrannical conquerors dates from this time
and has passed into Greek folklore. Certainly there are
numerous examples of such abuses and by the nineteenth
century Turkish indolence and inertia had produced effects of a
negative, wasting kind. But this was not the picture of Greece
during the earlier centuries of Turkish rule, and as far as the
majority of Greeks were concerned Ottoman rule had been
preferred to others. What the Greeks suffered from most was
not the strictness of Turkish rule, though taxes were heavy and
land scarce, but its laxity, inefficiency and corruption. The fact
that they imposed few general rules meant that the Greeks lived
according to their former customs and were adept at
manipulating the Turkish power wherever possible to their
own political and commercial advantage.

The Land

Ottoman rule was an absolute autocratic monarchy in which,
theoretically, all land belonged to the Sultan. Greece came
under the administration of the *Beglerbeg* (Lord of Lords) of
Roumeli (European Turkey) stationed at Sofia, and in 1470 its
lands comprised a number of *sanjaks* or *pashalics* organised on a
military basis and subdivided into a large number of *cazas* or
subdistricts. Within the provinces land was divided between
Turkish and Greek subjects, but the creation of large military
fiefs, run on a strict feudal pattern, meant that the Turkish
share was invariably larger than the Greek, and no land
assigned to Turkish ownership could pass into Greek hands. It
has been calculated that in the Peloponnesus the Turks had
eighteen times as much land per capita as the Greeks and the
Greek landowner could improve his individual situation only
at the expense of his fellow-Greeks. The notorious agrarian
malpractices, therefore, were not always the deeds of the Turks,
for Greek landowners, lay and ecclesiastical, were also

responsible for the downtrodden, underprivileged and tax-ridden Greek *rayahs*. The result was the creation of a large class of landless Greeks whose choice was either to work as serfs on the Greek and Turkish estates, lead a life of brigandage in the mountains, or to become merchant adventurers on the seas.

In many ways Greece was in a more fortunate position than most Balkan lands, for much of it was unsuited to the Turkish form of agricultural exploitation in which extensive grain and cotton cultivation played a major part. The Turks never fully controlled the mountainous and peninsular regions of the west and south, preferring instead the more easily accessible plains and basins of Macedonia, Thrace and Thessaly where their large estates or *chiflics* were worked by Greek serf labour. In effect these were large colonial plantations in which the closely controlled rural society had virtually no independence. The landowners received as much as one third of the farmers' produce, so there was little incentive to increase output which would merely inflate Turkish profits. It is not surprising, under such control, that Thessaly and northern Greece in general played a less active role in the initial stages of the War of Independence. Greek insurgence came from the more autonomous south and the *chifliki* conditions persisted in Thessaly until 1881 and in other parts of the north until well into the twentieth century.

Church and Government

Unlike earlier conquerors the Turks did not attempt any wholesale conversion of the Greeks to Islam but sought instead to rehabilitate the Orthodox Church, so long depressed by Rome, and utilise its organisation to manage the Greek population. Extensive conquests had made the empire a multi-racial society and the Turks were generally tolerant of other religions. Non-Moslem subjects, however, were anything but equals and separate religious communities known as *millets* were formed to administer them. Each had complete autonomy under the authority and leadership of an ecclesiastical functionary who was also given important temporal powers. Governed by their own laws, even when these differed from the

Turkish code, the *millets*, though not territorially defined, were nonetheless states within the state.

From both the cultural and commercial points of view the Ottoman administration greatly benefited the Greeks. The most influential head of the Turkish *millets* was the Orthodox Patriarch of Constantinople who, in addition to his religious duties, was a high Ottoman official responsible to the government for a wide range of administrative, legal and educational subjects. Technically he was the Greek national ruler – the *ethnarch* – and by the end of the eighteenth century he was the head of some 13 million Christians, one-quarter of the empire's inhabitants. In Constantinople he was assisted in his administrative duties by an ever-increasing class of educated and often extremely wealthy Greeks, many of whom moved on

Old Mosque, Ioannina

to specialist and diplomatic posts on the staff of the Sultan himself. These Phanariots, as they came to be known, were to play important moral and practical roles in the events leading to the Greek War of Independence (see Chapter 6).

It is not surprising that the Greek clergy preferred, in the words of Voltaire, 'the turban of a Turkish priest to the red hat of a Roman cardinal'. It is true that there were religious purges and oppressions, and many Christian churches, including Santa Sophia, were converted into mosques, but the fact remains that for Orthodoxy the Turkish regime was basically a tolerant one.

THE COURT OF ALI PASHA

The dependence of the Ottoman rulers on subject peoples to administer their lands was a useful, but at the same time a dangerous precedent. Inevitably, as central authority weakened, non-Moslems throughout the empire strained for independence. By the end of the eighteenth century the tolerant Turkish attitude had been replaced by one characterised by ruthless controls and outright oppression in an attempt to quell insurrection. It is from this time that commentaries speak of misery, squalor and slaughter in the empire, and as the movement for Greek independence gathered momentum massacres without cause ostensibly served as examples of what would follow if towns, districts or islands aided and abetted the revolutionaries. The empire also suffered from revolt amongst its own Moslem rulers who, with inflated ideas of grandeur, saw themselves as potential sultans. By the beginning of the nineteenth century Egypt under Mehemet Ali had become virtually independent of Constantinople and Ali Pasha in Epirus put up a spirited struggle for his own independence, an event which had major implications for Greek liberation.

Ali Pasha was born in 1741 in the Albanian village of Tepelin. His military services to the Sultan were rewarded in 1788 when he was given a pashalic based on Trikkala in the upper plain of Thessaly. Not content with this, and determined to relinquish his dependence on Constantinople, he quickly increased his domains and by 1807 ruled the whole of Epirus, Acarnania, Thessaly and Albania. Ioannina, with a population of around 35,000, became Ali's capital and consequently managed to retain throughout the Turkish period the cultural and commercial importance that had made it famous in the Middle Ages. It continued its role as a centre of Hellenism and its schools taught ancient Greek, Latin and French.

The Greeks, it seems, can suffer most forms of tyrannical government provided a profit motive is involved, and there is no denying that Ioannina reached its peak of commercial prestige under Ali Pasha. Yet no words can accurately describe his ruthless and sadistic reign of terror which was a continuum of murders, burnings, drownings, impalements, poisonings, mutilations and other butcheries of horrific proportions. These he planned from his strongly fortified Kastro (overlooking Ioannina's lake) whose great gates were usually ornamented by the crucified remains of his latest victims. Ali's inhuman perversions were inherited by his sons Mukhtar and Veli, the former's uncontrollable lust leading to raping excursions in broad daylight in Ioannina's streets and the latter the infamous possessor of the largest library of pornography in the Near East. Ali's sister, too, was not without her perversions and it is reported that she slept on mattresses stuffed with human hair from a great palace massacre engineered by her brother.

If the European powers were fully aware of the magnitude of Ali Pasha's monstrous deeds, they were forced for diplomatic reasons to turn a blind eye to them. Indeed, if anything, they pandered to Ali's whims since his lands, in a rapidly changing Ottoman empire, were of major strategic significance and later became one of the key areas in the subsequent Eastern Question. Britain, France and Russia appointed consuls to the court at Ioannina where reports of its oriental opulence with harems, eunuchs, pages, concubines, jewels, silks and magnificent feasts attracted great interest and many visitors. Ali, in spite of his savage cruelty, was a courteous and exquisite host and in 1809 entertained Byron and his companion John Cam Hobhouse. Byron knew of the Pasha's cruelties, but praised the hospitality of the court and stayed long enough to

An Athenian sponge-seller at Constitution Square*

In Athens, nineteenth-century neo-classical architecture is well represented by the Hellenic Academy. The central frieze is a copy from the Parthenon and the building is guarded by two large ionic columns surmounted by the figures of Athena and Apollo*

begin his *Childe Harold's Pilgrimage*. The British resident at the court was Colonel W. M. Leake, the great topographer of Greece, and Henry Holland was Ali Pasha's doctor.

Constantinople could not remain indefinitely indifferent to Ali's insurbordinate actions in Greece and when the Sultan learned of the attempted assassination of an official in his services he publicly deposed Ali and ordered his return to Constantinople. The Pasha, not unexpectedly, refused and the Sultan mobilised an army to go and fetch him. Besieged in his capital by Turkish troops for fifteen months and bereft of allies and most of his family, Ali's end was indeed dramatic. Forced to abandon the Kastro for the greater security of a pavilion on the island in the lake, Ali first bombarded the town from its batteries. Some Turks, landing on the island, broke into the room immediately below that in which Ali had barricaded himself. Firing through the ceiling Ali was hit and expired, it is said, breathing defiance and threats of revenge.

Ali Pasha's war with the Sultan was the incident for which the Greek insurgent forces had waited. At a time when Moslem was fighting Moslem on Greek soil it seemed an appropriate moment for the various bodies of freedom fighters to raise the banner for independence. Yet though events in Epirus had provided the vital opportunity for revolt the province was to remain under strong Turkish control and was not united with Greece until 1913 when, on 21 February, the Greek army entered Ioannina.

6

The Strands of Freedom

Though factors of the most varied origin contributed to the birth of modern Greece, their common linkage was the growth of national consciousness which, in the face of the increasingly repressive Turkish policies, received its greatest and most vigorous affirmation at the beginning of the nineteenth century. To the Greeks, as to the other Balkan peoples, nationalism meant the love of country and a strong feeling of ethnic-religious unity. Both had been sustained throughout the centuries of Turkish occupation, partly by the closely knit Greek family system and partly by the teachings of the Orthodox Church which promoted Greek traditions and language as vital ethnic links. The renewal of national awareness was fostered and fed by a cultural and intellectual renaissance in which writers and other scholars kindled positive reaction among the most diverse peoples of the Greek world. These included illiterate and poverty-stricken peasants (many of which had taken to a life of lawlessness in the Peloponnesus and other mountainous provinces), merchant mariners of the Aegean coasts and islands, the urban bourgeoisie and Orthodox prelates in Constantinople and other Ottoman cities, and a varied assortment of intense and often eccentric philhellenes throughout Europe who gave both moral and practical support to the Greek cause. Inevitably, all tried to lead the revolution in different directions but though divergences of views created rifts and tensions within and between these Greek worlds, cumulatively they produced a heightened sense of national consciousness and a confidence in the viability of a Greek state.

THE POET-POLITICIANS

By the turn of the century the Greek national movement had become firmly tied to the ferment of ideas produced by the European Enlightenment and the French Revolution and through the medium of refugee or expatriate intellectuals the rallying cry of 'Liberty and Freedom' found a response in Greece. Constantine Rhigas (1760–98), also known as Rhigas Pheraios, occupies the honoured place of precursor in the history of Greece's struggle for national and social liberation. This fiery Vlach poet from Valestino (ancient Pherai) in Thessaly travelled widely in Europe dispensing revolutionary doctrines and seeking support for a free Greece based on the French model constitution of the 1790s. Believing that the influence of revolutionary France would shortly lead to action in the Balkans, Rhigas moved to Vienna where members of the large Greek community helped him to organise an abortive conspiracy to overthrow the Turkish regime. In Vienna he published translations of foreign works in the Greek demotic or common tongue and assembled a collection of national songs of which the most famous was his Greek version of the Marseillaise, paraphrased by Byron as 'Sons of the Greeks, arise'. Rhigas' songs were published posthumously, for in 1797 he was arrested by the Austrians in Trieste and delivered to the Turks who failed to appreciate his revolutionary messages and disruptive calls:

How long, my heroes, shall we live in bondage,
alone like lions on ridges, on peaks?
Living in caves, seeing our children
turned from the land to bitter enslavement?
Losing our land, brothers and parents,
our friends, our children and all our relations?
Better an hour of life that is free
than forty years in slavery.

On 24 June 1798, Rhigas was strangled (or shot) at Belgrade and his body is said to have been cast into the Danube, though its confluence the Sava is also mentioned. The story goes that before he perished Rhigas said: 'This is how brave men die. I have sown; soon will come the hour when my nation will gather the ripe fruit.'

Rhigas was undoubtedly the forerunner of the Greek revolution, but there were other illuminists eager to propagate the cause. Such was Adamantios Korais (1748–1833), the son of a rich Smyrna merchant, who after studying at Montpellier, settled in Paris in 1788. Unlike the volatile Rhigas, Korais was a contemplative scholar and an apostle of evolution rather than revolution. A prolific writer, editor and translator, he laid great stress on Greece's classical heritage and attempted to bridge the gap, which had increasingly widened over the centuries, between the written and the demotic language. This was of more than academic interest for the codifying of the written language, as in other Balkan countries, was a powerful factor in the birth of the new nation. Korais set himself the task of reconstructing a literary Greek language which would combine the best elements of the ancient and modern tongues, removing in the process all foreign accretions. The result of his systematisation was *katharevousa*, a purified, artificial language which though adopted as the official language after liberation was little understood at the lower social levels.

Not surprisingly *katharevousa* had its opponents, particularly the poets and other writers of the Ionian islands, where the Greek cultural renaissance was conducted from a safe political arena. Britain had seized the islands from France in 1814 and under the protection of George III set up The United States of the Ionian Islands governed by a lord high commissioner. They remained a protectorate until 1864 and, largely shielded from the political upheavals of the adjacent Greek mainland, prospered both materially and culturally. One school of writers collected folksongs to feed Greek patriotism with memories of its past glory and heroism, whilst another paved the way to freedom by regarding education as the key to the destiny of their fellow-countrymen. The Ionian writers worked in the popular demotic tongue, but both 'language schools' were symptoms of the Greek educational revival and of the new feeling of nationalism.

The most notable Ionian poet was Dionysios Solomos (1798–1857) who was born in Zakinthos but spent most of his life in Corfu. Solomos elevated the demotic language to a refined artistic medium capable of expressing with simplicity and power his feelings for nature and for the recurrent themes of revolutionary Greece – freedom, truth, love and death: the opening stanzas of his *Ode to Liberty* were adopted as the Greek national anthem. Solomos was later influenced by Byron to whom he addressed a famous ode, but reputedly his greatest poem, though incomplete, was *The Free Besieged*, an epic providing a dramatic and symbolic setting to the Siege of Missolonghi. Notable contemporaries of Solomos were Andreas Kalvos and Aristoteles Valaoritis, the former the author of lyrics of great beauty and the latter a romantic writer who also championed demoticism and modelled his verse on the patriotic ballads of the klephts (see below).

The Ionian islands undoubtedly made a considerable contribution in preparing the ground for the Greek revolution, and not only through their poets and writers. Having escaped Ottoman domination, they were, in theory at least, an independent Greek state. Yet the islands were neither large enough nor rich enough to become the 'piedmont' of the liberation and, furthermore, they were too firmly controlled by Britain to play a leading role when the revolution began. British policy was one of enforcing a precarious neutrality to the events of the mainland though in practice this was done in a half-hearted manner. Escape to the Ionian islands was the most promising way home for Europeans actively engaged in the Greek cause, and Corfu, in particular, became a refuge for Greeks fleeing from Turkish reprisals. Subsequently, however, the cultural maturity and political experience of the leading Ionian families were to provide illustrious recruits to the political and administrative ranks of the Greek state. Chief of these was Count John Capodistrias, a leading figure in the history of modern Greece and destined to become the country's first elected president. His house is a national monument in Corfu town and his remains are buried in a simple tomb in the nearby seventeenth-century Platytera monastery.

PHILHELLENES AND PHANARIOTS

As the movement to recover and renew a submerged national culture accelerated, its fundamental aim for the liberation of Hellas became a cause fervently supported by philhellenes throughout Europe. In the beginning these were the young and educated, most of them again poets and writers who looked upon the Greek crusade as an exciting enterprise and a highly emotional romance. 'We are all Greeks', Shelley wrote in 1821, 'our laws, our literature, our arts have their roots in Greece', and Hugo and Schiller held similar views. But the philhellenic movement produced its greatest hero in George Gordon, Lord Byron (1788–1824), whose impression remains indelibly stamped on Greece today. He is remembered not merely in the monuments and memorials to him, but also in the name Vyron, the hellenised form, which many Greeks bear. Largely on account of his fame (or infamy) the role of the philhellenes in the Greek revolution has been romantically exaggerated, but the legend of the heroic poet who fought and died for freedom was to inspire countless generations.

Byron's introduction to Greece was in 1809 when, at the age of twenty-two, he made his first eastern journey, taking refuge from England where he had been generally condemned for his reckless life. After landing in Epirus and visiting Ioannina, Prevenza, Patras and Delphi, he arrived in Athens and in ten weeks, aided no doubt by his professed attraction to three young Greek girls, learned a fair amount of modern Greek. Bryon's first-hand experiences of Greece and his perceptive understanding of the rebellion and the rebels were in striking contrast to the views held by the London Committee formed in March 1823 to aid the Greek cause. Its membership had grown to 400 within a year and included a broad spectrum of influential people, giving it much publicity as well as a later notoriety. From Italy Byron accepted the Committee's request to act as its agent in Greece and much of his work involved the problems of moderating the suspicious and undisciplined tactics of the Greek chiefs and of discouraging the often impractical schemes proposed from London. Byron's untimely death at Missolonghi had the effect of transforming the philhellenic movement into an international crusade. Society tea parties and other fund-raising ventures became fashionable throughout western Europe and even in Poland and America; in Vienna a cultural society known as the 'Friends of the Muses' received contributions from the Tsar, Talleyrand and Metternich.

There was another society working for the Greek cause that had little in common with drawing-room tea parties. Its title, the Friendly Society (Philiki Etairia), was a misnomer, for developing out of the prosperous Greek trading colony of Odessa in 1814, it was conspiratorial, highly secretive and had bizarre initiation ceremonies. Greek landowners, bishops, mountain bandits, merchants and sea captains formed its membership and recruitment was accelerated when the society moved its headquarters to Constantinople. It failed, however, to attract the support of Count John Capodistrias, though his brothers Argostino and Viaro were active members.

Constantinople was still the centre of the Greek imperial world where an administrative aristocracy had developed among the Greek officials known as Phanariots. The term was derived from the north-western corner of the city – the lighthouse or phanar district – where the Patriarch had established his headquarters, though the district also became the preserve of Greek merchants as well as clergy. By the nineteenth century these highly educated merchants with a first-hand knowledge of western customs and languages had risen to the topmost ranks in the Ottoman bureaucracy with titles such as Grand Vizier and Grand Dragoman. Their powers were reinforced by the Orthodox clergy and by the crowds of lesser Greek officials that surrounded them. Prince Alexander Ipsilantes, a Phanariot Greek whose father had been *hospodar* of Moldavia and Wallachia, resigned his career in the Russian army where he had been a major-general and aide-de-camp to the Tsar, to become the General Commissioner of the Friendly Society. Its plan was the overthrow of the Turkish regime through a number of concerted uprisings in Epirus, the Peloponnesus, central Greece and the islands. For its success

local peasant involvement was a prerequisite, emphasising the
fact that though masterminded by the intelligentsia and the
bourgeoisie the Greek revolution was much more than a simple
class affair.

THE ROBBER-GENERALS

The Greek literary and intellectual renaissance, the high ideals
of the philhellenes and the commercial and other support of
the urban Greeks all stood in marked contrast to the
unsophisticated but equally positive patriotism of the Greek
peasant world. The Greeks, as already noted, retained a
considerable amount of administrative freedom under
Ottoman rule, and the Peloponnesus, in particular, was
virtually an autonomous region. Here the Turkish occupation
amounted to little more than a military presence in certain
towns and strongholds and the Greeks outnumbered the
Moslems by 400,000 to 40,000. Together with the Aegean
islands, where Turkish rule had never been effective, the
Peloponnesus formed an integral part of insurgent Greece,
where a fighting spirit had been maintained by the *klephts* and
the *armatoloi*.

The klephts, whose name literally meant robbers, were
mountain-adventurers, half brigands, half patriots, who
refused to acknowledge Turkish suzerainty. The armatoloi
were Greek militiamen enrolled for the policing of districts to
counter the activities of klephtic bands who were not adverse to
raiding their fellow countrymen, referring to them as servants
of the Turks. Some of the more powerful bands came to terms
with the Turks and were granted rights of autonomy as tribal
chiefs and the powers to form their own armed militia for self-
preservation, particularly for the protection of dependent
villages which supplied them, almost in Mexican bandit
fashion, with food and other necessities. When the Turks began
to reassert their authority both klephts and armatoloi found
themselves opposing and harassing the conqueror. With the
outbreak of the War of Independence there was little difference
between them and both came to incarnate the spirit of Greek

resistance and collectively they constituted the land forces.

Theodoros Kolokotronis (1770–1863) was one of the outstanding figures of the war and the leader of the insurrection in the Peloponnesus. Equestrian statues of him stand in Athens and Nauplia, though his volatile character brought him imprisonment, sentence of death and pardon before these honours were conferred. George Karaiskakis (1780–1827) also proved himself a great military leader, especially at the battle of Phaleron which cost him his life. Another hero, mourned equally for his modesty, was Marcos Botsaris (1790–1823) who first fought for the cause of Suliot freedom against Ali Pasha before joining his compatriots at Missolonghi. Many klephts suffered horrible deaths at the hands of the Turks. Such a fate befell Athanasios Diakos (1788–1821) who put up the epic defence of the Alamana bridge, across the Sperchios. Wounded, he was captured by the Turks and taken to Lamia where on 23 April 1821 he was impaled and roasted on a spit. It is little wonder that the dying urge of a klepht was for his companions to cut off his head to avoid it falling into Turkish hands. The Turkish custom was to expose the severed heads to view in their towns and fortresses.

The War of Independence made the klephts heroes and in characteristic Greek fashion subsequent generations have surrounded them with a body of myth and legend – on a par with Robin Hood or the Scottish Rob Roy – where they are extolled as brave, generous and resolute fighters of oppression. Their ballads – *klephtika* – undoubtedly sung by their camp fires in true outlaw tradition, ring with the ideas of freedom, estranged love and death. They have now passed, heavily coated with romantic whitewash, into the repertory of Greek national folksongs, many of them myrologia or dirges. Such themes still colour popular music, often made all the more plaintive by the timorous strains of the bouzouki.

Many exploits of the klephts, exaggeratedly portrayed, have survived in the *Karaghiosis*, the traditional country shadow shows not unlike Punch and Judy or the Kasperle-Theater of Germany. They are played with cardboard figures moved by sticks, whose shadows are projected, to the accompaniment of a dialogue and music, on to an illuminated and often highly decorated screen. Though now less common as a result of mass-produced entertainment, these shows are still a feature at travelling fairs and local festivals, attracting young and old alike. Their freely adapted story lines maintain certain conventions, particularly in the character of Karaghiosis himself. This vain mischievious hunchback with large sensuous nose and big black moustache is undoubtedly Turkish inspired. Yet he is also the epitome of Greek *philotimo* or self-pride, living on his wits to avoid the debt-collectors and other officials. His cunning never fails to get the better of all his opponents. The stories and myths in which Karaghiosis is portrayed seem to embrace at least 3,000 years of Greek history, but the Turkish occupation and the exploits of the mountain heroes provide him with the most colourful and entertaining of dialogues. Hunchback aside, he can almost be taken for the heavily moustachioed Kolokotronis but some of his characteristics seem borrowed from Alexander the Great.

The klephts were also responsible for popularising the colourful dress now accepted as the country's male national costume, though traditionally it derives from southern Albania where it was greatly admired by Byron. The red fez or tasselled skull cap, elaborately embroidered jacket and white pleated skirt or fustanella (which might have originated from the tunics of the Roman legionaires stationed in Illyria), are today the bases of the Evzone uniform, the Greek élite soldier guard. Such sartorial elegance, complete with Turkish slippers and white ballerina-type stockings, belies the proud battle honours of this light infantry. Like the klephts before them, the evzones have earned a privileged place in the military history of modern Greece.

THE MERCHANT-CORSAIRS

What the klephts were achieving on the mainland was complemented by the Greek (and Albanian) merchant skippers who from island territories such as Hydra, Spetses and Psara (known as the Naval Islands) combined to harry Turkish shipping, an occupation that became a Greek naval pastime. The Greeks had always been better mariners than the Turks and most of the seaborne trade of the Ottoman empire was run by them. They were pirates too and the sea captains and ship-owners could acquire large fortunes. Armed with perhaps a dozen cannon and equipped with no more than a hundred men apiece, the swift Greek brigs soon made a hornets' nest of the Aegean. With little to fear from a Turkish navy manned by unreliable Greek crews and commanded by Turkish officers largely ignorant of the sea, the Greek merchants perfected a deadly weapon which proved to be one of the most successful of the war. It was an expendable vessel the inside of which was crammed with powder kegs and daubed with pitch, turpentine and sulphur, as was the rigging. Appearing at night from the secret coves that festoon the Aegean, these ships were steered down on the enemy vessels and the powder train set alight leaving the Turks to fight both fire and the sea.

Each of the Naval Islands had admirals whose heroic deeds have gone down in Greek history and whose memories are perpetuated in the names of streets, squares and wharves in the majority of Greek ports. On Psara, the small island near Chios, it was Constantine Canaris (1790–1877) whose dexterity with fire-ships won him admiration throughout Europe. In June 1822, soon after the massacre of Chios when the Turks killed or sold into slavery almost all of the island's 100,000 inhabitants, Canaris commanded such a fire-ship and it blew up the Turkish flagship and almost all the Turkish captains as they were gathered aboard to celebrate the end of Ramadan. The Chios slaughter become the subject of a painting, 'The Massacre at Chios', by Delacroix which together with Byron's appeal from Missolonghi did much to prompt the conscience of the west. Canaris survived his daring naval strategies to become prime minister of Greece several times, the last occasion when he was extremely advanced in years.

But for the islanders of Spetses, no one could outshine Admiral Lascarina Bouboulina, not least because she was a woman. Taking her name from that of her second husband, she led a number of sea and land battles before being assassinated at Spetses. The whole of the Argolid coast and its attendant islands remember her bravery but though her statue in Nauplia is romantically flattering, some of her exploits are recalled with savage chauvinist humour, not uncommon to the Greek male. It is said that Bouboulina could outdrink any man and so unattractive was this nineteenth-century Amazon that her lovers were seduced at gunpoint!

Chief of all the naval centres, however, was the waterless and barren Argo-Saronic island of Hydra, uninhabited throughout classical times and for the first fourteen centuries of our era. By the seventeenth century Hydra had developed a remarkable capability for adventurous, often piratical, trading, earning for itself the title 'Venice of the Aegean'. It had in fact been one of the small ports in the Venetian empire chain, but its leading mercantile families were of Albanian descent whose forebears had fled from the Turks in Epirus and elsewhere. They quickly profited from the growth of trade between Asia Minor, the Levant and Egypt and the fast 15 ton trading vessel, the *sakturia*, not unlike the Greek caique seen today throughout the Aegean, plied the waters of the eastern Mediterranean and the Black Sea. Another of the island's vessels was the lateen-rigged *latinadika*, which traded as far as France, Spain, Portugal and even to the West Indies and the estuary of the Rio de la Plata. An enormous contraband trade developed during the Napoleonic Wars with ships running the British blockade and by the time of the War of Independence, Hydra with 124 ships had reached the peak of prosperity. Of its estimated population of 28,000, almost half were seafarers and one family alone was estimated as being worth two million pounds sterling.

It was from Hydra that the raiding parties of Tsamados and Tombasis sailed, supported by their own fortunes and the wealth of other trading families such as Boundouris, Voulgaris and Koudouriotos. But the hero of Hydra was undoubtedly Andreas Miaoulis (1769–1835), a Euboean by birth who had served an apprenticeship with the Barbary corsairs. He, too, used his own fortune in the cause of Greek independence, defeating the Turkish fleet several times and in 1825 supplying the besieged town of Missolonghi. To the Greeks Miaoulis was their Nelson, though a comparison with the earlier privateering activities of Sir Francis Drake would be more appropriate. Yet even great admirals can make mistakes and in the political confusion that surrounded the war's initial success, Miaoulis in 1831, using the methods he had perfected, set fire to the Greek fleet anchored at neighbouring Poros. He died, aged sixty-six, in Athens in 1835.

In view of Hydra's contribution to Greek liberation it was an unjust reward that changing conditions of trade and the advent of the steamboat should favour other ports, notably Syros in the Cyclades and subsequently Piraeus. Hydra's commerce rapidly declined though its former glory is still reflected in the architecture of the town, and many of the houses, some now museums or put to other uses, contain legacies of the wealth acquired as the result of trade – Italian paintings, Venetian glass, tapestries, fine mahogany furniture and all the elegance of late eighteenth-century Europe. Yet the presence in these large mansions of store-houses, water cisterns and even bakeries indicates that they were also designed as miniature fortresses, capable of resisting prolonged siege. Miaoulis' cannon still guards the harbour and in June the town celebrates the *Miaoulia* festival when for one day at least the tourists who now monopolise the town in the summer months are subordinated to the pride of Hydra's illustrious past.

MISSOLONGHI AND NAVARINO

The date given for the official uprising of the Greeks against Turkish rule, and still celebrated as Independence Day, is 25 March 1821, when Germanos, Metropolitan Bishop of Patras, is reputed to have raised the standard of revolt at the tenth-century monastery of Aghia Lavra. The savage conflict, in spite of Ottoman weakness, lasted until 1829 and was accompanied by great destruction and many atrocities in which vengeance, greed, hunger for power and simple blood lust all played their part. Yet at the same time the war was marked by feats of great bravery on the part of both Greek and Turkish forces.

By 1823 the insurgents had almost succeeded in clearing

southern Greece and its waters from Turkish forces, but, lacking self-discipline, their petty quarrels over territories and leadership led to serious civil strife and ultimately to anarchy. An assembly at Epidauros on 13 January 1822 had proclaimed Greek independence and elected the Phanariot Alexander Mavrokordato as president. But the military chiefs and other rival bodies resented any attempts to form a regular government and in the confusion that followed the Turks returned, and with Egyptian help reconquered almost the whole of the Greek-controlled territory.

North of the Gulf of Corinth the lagoon town of Missolonghi, with some 5,000 defenders, held out, and betwen May 1825 and April 1826 was besieged by a combined Turco-Egyptian army. It was here that Lord Byron died, together with many other volunteers from abroad, for with supplies exhausted, sickness and pestilence further reduced the resources of the town. A letter written by a Swiss volunteer named Meyer and smuggled through the siege lines graphically describes the conditions:

> We are reduced to feed upon the most disgusting animals . . . we are suffering horribly from hunger and thirst . . . Sickness adds much to the calamities which overwhelm us . . . we have been terribly distressed by the cold, for we have suffered a great want of wood. Notwithstanding so many privations it is a . . . noble spectacle to witness the ardour and devotedness of the garrison.

After twelve months' siege and with all supplies gone the defenders, escorting their women and children, attempted to break through the enemy lines on the night of 22–3 April 1826. Known as the *exodus*, the majority perished in the attempt and those who remained in the town fired their magazines, overwhelming themselves and their enemies in a common destruction.

Missolonghi marked the turning-point in the War of Independence for the heroic resistance and ultimate fall of the town made a tremendous impression on all Europe, arousing universal sympathy for the Greek cause. The possibility of foreign intervention was at last taking shape and the Treaty of

London (6 July 1827) provided that Britain, France and Russia should guarantee the autonomy of Greece under the suzerainty of Turkey, without breaking off friendly relations with the Porte. Turkey's refusal to accept such a suggestion led to the arrival, in the Bay of Navarino in the south-west Peloponnesus, of an allied fleet of 11 British, 8 Russian and 7 French ships whose brief, under the direction of the senior admiral Codrington, was the 'peaceful intimidation' of the Turkish forces to withdraw. On 20 October a few nervous shots fired by the Turks precipitated a general action in which the Turkish fleet was annihilated. Metternich called it a 'frightful catastrophe' and Wellington termed it an 'untoward event'; few people in Europe were unduly distressed by the Turkish defeat. What now became of major significance, however, was the future status of Greece for though sovereignty was assured it had not been won by Greece itself.

At an assembly near ancient Troizen in May 1827 John Capodistrias had been elected the new Greek president though the title *kyvernitis*, literally meant governor. His appointment reflected the need to secure foreign confidence in Greece for Capodistrias had had wide experience in international politics. His main problem was curbing petty factionalism, but in spite of initial success he was unable to overcome regional animosity, especially among the mountain chiefs. A violent dispute with the militant clans of the Mani in the southern Peloponnesus culminated in his assassination at Nauplia on 9 October 1831. Capodistrias' death was followed by a period of open civil war when Britain, France and Russian forces again intervened in the affairs of Greece. Convinced that Greece should become an independent monarchy, the allies undertook the task of finding it a ruler. In May 1832, the Greek crown was accepted by King Ludwig I of Bavaria, an enthusiastic philhellene, on behalf of his younger son Otho, who was only seventeen when he arrived in Greece. From Corfu, where he had been entertained by the British High Commissioner Lord Nugent, a fleet of Bavarian troops escorted him to Nauplia, the provisional capital.

7

Country and Capital

King Otho's kingdom, the first united and independent Greece in history, was small both in area and in population. It consisted of the Peloponnesus, the southern part of the main peninsula known as Sterea Hellas, the large island of Euboea and the smaller islands of the northern Sporades and Cyclades groups. The inclusion of the Cyclades was the outcome of considerable debate on the part of the Great Powers, but France was eager to protect the Catholic communities on Naxos, Tinos, Thera and Syros – the survivors from Frankish days – and Syros had also been a refuge for many of the Greeks that escaped from the massacre in Chios, an event which, as previously stated, had quickened the conscience of the West. In total, however, Greek territory approximated to one-third of the country's present size and of its 753,000 people, 95 per cent were peasant farmers belonging to an archaic, semi-feudal structure.

The new state was given as short a land frontier as was practicable and on 21 July 1832 it was fixed as a line from the Gulf of Arta in the west to the Gulf of Volos in the east, following the crest of the Othrys Mountains for part of its course. Though the Greeks refused to regard this frontier as permanent, it is significant that it had both physical and historical integrity, for it closely followed the transitional zone which in antiquity had demarcated the essential Greek and Mediterranean world from the more continental areas to the north which were regarded as Hellenised rather than truly Greek in character.

Greece's nationalist and territorial ambitions were far from satisfied by these 1832 boundaries. The embryo state's peninsular and mountainous character included little

(*left*) Greek architecture
spans centuries of civilisation
as this ornamental balcony
in Athens, an example of
nineteenth-century
'Othonian' style, testifies;*
(*below*) the Greek Orthodox
church carries on the
traditions of the Byzantine
empire into modern Greece
and colourful ritual
accompanies celebrations
and services. At the
monastery of Iviron on
Mount Athos the important
feast of *Panaghia Portraitissa* is
celebrated on 15 August*

(*above*) Store keeper in
Ioannina;* (*right*) Greek
bread seller at Piraeus*

productive land, especially land suitable for cereals, and the division of the Aegean – traditionally a Greek sea – excluding many of the islands (including Crete), also proved unacceptable; such a division further hindered the highly important maritime traffic on which the new state was to depend. Essentially there were now two Greek communities – the territorial and the extra-territorial – and throughout the nineteenth century and until the Lausanne Treaty of 1923, Greek politics were preoccupied with the liberation of the Greek-inhabited regions still under Turkish control. This was an era of pan-Hellenic propaganda to which everything else in foreign and domestic policy became secondary. Irredentism was a profoundly unifying force and its main ideological and political slogan was preached throughout the Greek lands as the 'Great Idea'. Its torch was carried by monarchs and politicians, including Otho, but more importantly by Eleutherios Venizelos, the Cretan-born statesman who worked both for the union of his native island with Greece and for the greater aim of consolidating the Greek people as they had been territorially and culturally united under the Byzantine empire. In these grandiose ambitions, which were all but realised in the 1920s, Constantinople featured prominently.

THE CAPITAL

Whereas many Greeks were prepared to wait optimistically for the emancipation of Constantinople, the infant kingdom was in need of a capital city to centralise government and administration in a country of immature political factions. The revolution had left a devastated landscape, for not only had over 200,000 people lost their lives, agricultural land had been destroyed wholesale, and provincial towns, including Thebes, Patras, Athens, Tripolis, Corinth and Kalamata, were in complete ruins. The destruction of Patras was particularly unfortunate because by fully utilising the commercial traditions bequeathed it by the Venetians it had become, by the early nineteenth century, a flourishing port city and one of the few places in Greece that had foreign consuls and, hence, some

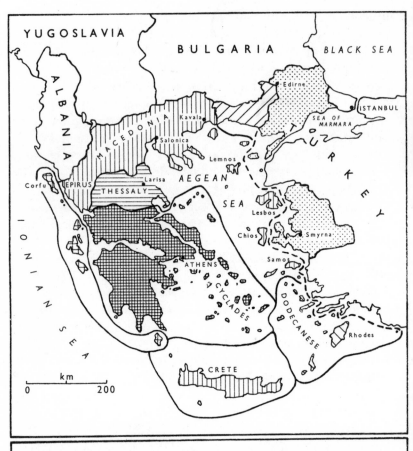

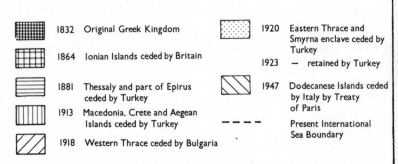

TERRITORIAL GROWTH OF GREECE

	1832	Original Greek Kingdom
	1864	Ionian Islands ceded by Britain
	1881	Thessaly and part of Epirus ceded by Turkey
	1913	Macedonia, Crete and Aegean Islands ceded by Turkey
	1918	Western Thrace ceded by Bulgaria
	1920	Eastern Thrace and Smyrna enclave ceded by Turkey
	1923 —	retained by Turkey
	1947	Dodecanese Islands ceded by Italy by Treaty of Paris
- - - -		Present International Sea Boundary

Territorial growth of Greece

view of the outside world. It was burned and sacked by the Turks in 1821 and the grid plan of the present city with its attractive arcaded streets is largely the result of a building programme inaugurated by Capodistrias.

The choice of Nauplia as a provisional capital was more than fortuitous for, wrested from the Turks early in the War of Independence, it was the only sizeable settlement that had escaped severe destruction. The modern town, though unmistakably provincial, is obviously proud of the part it played in early Greek national life and its general character and atmosphere still retains something of its brief nineteenth-century glory. Streets bear the names of Greek kings and their consorts as well as those of the heroes of the war; there are also statues, equestrian and otherwise, to Kolokotronis, Ipsilantis, Bouboulina and Capodistrias. The latter's assassination while attending the church of St Spiridion (ironically the patron saint of his native Corfu) remains Nauplia's greatest shame.

In the selection of a permanent capital nominations came not only from Nauplia and Patras, but also from cities such as Corinth, Tripolis, Argos and Syros (Ermopoulis) – any settlement, in fact, that felt it had some historical or contemporary claim to the title. The Greek army, and many statesmen, would have preferred the continuation of Nauplia (if it 'were cleaned up') but it was the historical claim of Athens and pressures from King Ludwig that finally prevailed to make Athens the choice. Ironically, it was one of the most provincial, and certainly the least wealthy, of Greek towns and though to contrast nineteenth-century Athens with Constantinople is a little unrealistic it is nonetheless revealing. The latter, as the seat of the Patriarchate and the centre of the Greek bourgeoisie, remained the symbol of Greek national and religious regeneration. Its Greek population amounted to over 200,000 and it housed numerous Hellenic schools, publishing houses and a university of high prestige. When Athens was chosen as capital it was in a wretched state and was little more than a ruined Turkish-style market town with a population variously estimated between 2,000 and 10,000. The settlement, surrounded by a light Turkish wall, clung to the northern and

eastern slopes of the acropolis hill and graphic descriptions of
its derelict state are provided by nineteenth-century visitors. In
1837, C. Wordsworth was prompted to comment that

> there is scarcely a building in Athens in so perfect a state as the
> Temple of Theseus, and the least ruined objects here are some of
> the ruins themselves. The streets are almost deserted, nearly all the
> houses are without roofs . . . a few new wooden houses and the two
> lines of planked sheds which form the bazaar are all the inhabited
> dwellings which Athens can now boast.

When Mure visited Athens in 1842 some rebuilding had taken
place but this he regarded 'as pearls in a dung hill, scattered
here and there at wide intervals among the cottages and ruins'.
These conditions were echoed in Piraeus which had declined
even further, for as early as the seventeenth century Wheeler
could state that 'the town that was here in former times is now
utterly ruined and deserted . . . the only building that now
remains is a kind of warehouse to receive merchandise and to
gather customs and taxes'.

Othonian Athens
The designation of Athens as capital in the absence of any
developed or commercially significant Greek centre proved in
time to be a sound choice and confirmed a statement appearing
in a German newspaper in 1832 that 'the site has excellent
advantages for the development of commerce toward any
direction and Athens in a few years can grow and prosper'. The
city was again destined to become the magnet of Greece – the
political capital and the centre of the nation's culture as well as
of its trade, industry and commerce. But its transformation into
a major city and its attainment of metropolitan respectability
under the Bavarian monarchy were slow processes and the city
soon became a target of international satire. Although Athens
acquired its opera-house as early as 1839, carriages in the city
were for some time unknown or, at least, very rare. There are
reports of fashionable ladies being taken to the opera on
donkeys, whose braying constantly disturbed performances.
Even by 1900 Athens was still regarded as provincial in its

habits and lacking in most of the amenities regarded as essentials in the West. It had no proper piped water supply, suffered from the lack of surfaced roads, was plagued by dust and wind, and hypercritical visitors ridiculed the incongruous, though undoubtedly picturesque, sight of peasants in fustanella costume driving their animals and carts laden with produce down boulevards lined with shining new marble buildings.

These boulevards formed part of the new Othonian Athens, an attempt chiefly on the part of the Bavarian and Greek architect-planners, Schaubert and Cleanthes, to develop the character of the city in a manner befitting its new status. After considerable local reaction and various revisions, the new Athens emerged in the form of a geometric street pattern centred on two large squares, Omonia and Constitution. The former, three-quarters of a mile to the north of the acropolis and the old settlement, formed the apex of a triangular arrangement of streets consisting of Piraeus, Stadium and Hermes Streets, with the latter forming the main artery of the old quarter. The triangle was bisected by Athinas Street and parallel to it Eolou was laid out, later to be continued as the great north road, Patission. Other major thoroughfares were Venizelos and Academias Streets, built parallel to Stadium. This inner structure, which remains unaltered today, formed the guidelines for subsequent urban expansion which took the form of a series of regular grid-iron blocks with orientations related to the central bases. By 1840 the plans for Piraeus had also been approved and it is interesting that its redevelopment followed principles strongly reminiscent of its classical predecessor.

Otho's Palace

Otho, accustomed to a Bavarian climate, was anxious to select a healthy site for the erection of the royal palace. An earlier suggestion by the Berlin architect Carl Schinkel to place it on the acropolis was mercifully rejected and after Bavarian officials had been despatched to sleep in various quarters of the city to sample nocturnal atmospheres a site was chosen above Constitution Square, then known as Boubounistra after an old fountain. Apparently it was found that the courtiers awoke here with lighter heads and more energy. The original neo-classical style for the palace was drawn up by Klentze, the Bavarian court architect, but for economic reasons his grandiose scheme was somewhat adapted and the work executed by his pupil Friedrich Gaertner, the foundation stone being laid by King Ludwig in 1836. The plain rather dull quadrangle-shaped building, with numerous windows and a Doric portico on its western front, was completed in 1842 and behind it and to its south-east the royal gardens, still a favourite Athenian retreat from the intensity of the summer sun, were laid out to the designs of Queen Amalia, Otho's consort.

From the date of its completion, the palace (now the Greek parliament house) was the focus of many rowdy political demonstrations. Bavarian rule was unpopular and many local factions kept alive the tradition of insurrection for many years. Initially Greece was governed by Bavarian regents until Otho's coming of age in 1835 when he presided in person over a cabinet hand-picked by his court. He was a pedantic and autocratic ruler and a bloodless coup was needed in 1843 to 'persuade' him to grant modern Greece's first constitution – hence the name of the square that fronts the palace. This outward show of democracy, however, failed to disguise Otho's despotic, and Amalia's impulsive, tendencies and Greek dissatisfaction with their monarchy culminated in another bloodless coup in October 1862 when Otho was deposed by his army – a precedent to be followed many times in the country's modern political history. They left Greece in the same month and retired to Bamberg in Bavaria where, four years later, ex-king Otho died.

In fairness, it should be said that Otho's reign had created a stronger Greece and one less dependent on foreign powers. The fact that no new territories were won for Greece, though Otho was an ardent supporter of irredentism, was a major factor in his downfall. The condition of Athens had considerably improved during Othonian rule since following in royalty's footsteps was as much a nineteenth-century Greek characteristic as aping the habits of Queen Victoria had been a favourite British pastime. Many wealthy Greeks from the provinces built their town houses in the capital and rich patrons from abroad contributed, as in Hellenistic and Roman times, to the architectural embellishment of the city, thereby enhancing its status as a capital. Baron Sina of Vienna, George Averoff of Alexandria, Theodore Tositas of Epirus and Andreas Syngros of Constantinople were among the benefactors who, between 1840 and 1890, commissioned public buildings for Athens. Schaubert and Cleanthes were involved in many of the designs, as was their compatriot Christian Hansen who was responsible for the first university. This, together with the National Library and the Hellenic Academy, built in a group in Venizelos or University Street, gave Athens a civic centre in the best of nineteenth-century neo-classical pretension. Similar buildings punctuated other parts of the townscape and the additional embassies, theatres and foreign schools, particularly of archaeology, greatly aided the transition from provincial to metropolitan status.

Othonian domestic architecture, though still incorporating neo-classical traditions, was far less pretentious. Basically its style was one of stuccoed façades incorporating the liberal use of ornamental balconies, balustrades, pilasters and other flourishes, and it provided a distinctive and environmentally successful style. Unfortunately, large sections of Othonian Athens have been redeveloped and its buildings replaced by the ubiquitous concrete and glass blocks common to most modern cities. Yet there are still many residences which exhibit many of the good qualities of the early period.

TERRITORIAL EXPANSION

At first the population of Athens expanded less than expected. The 1853 census records a figure of just 30,590 and in 1861, at the close of Otho's reign, it was only 41,298. The opening, in 1869, of the Athens-Piraeus railway, which was the first in Greece, greatly encouraged urban expansion along its route, particularly at New Phaleron on the Saronic coast, and the Attica railway, established around 1885, led to development towards the north at Halandri, Maroussi, Patissia and the fashionable suburb of Kifissia. But it was the Greek acquisition of new territories that was responsible for the rapid growth of the capital and towards the end of the century its population was around 180,000.

Though Greece ultimately acquired almost all the islands of the Aegean, boundary extensions in the nineteenth and early twentieth centuries were primarily northwards. Whereas in classical times provinces like Thessaly and Epirus were border regions between Greece proper and the 'barbarian' world, so these provinces and lands further north were gained in a piecemeal fashion, some by negotiation and agreement, others through hostilities and bitter diplomatic exchanges. Slowly the Greek jigsaw began to fall into place and the country trebled its original size and added to its population many thousands of people of Greek background or extraction. Yet in the course of this territorial expansion other ethnic groups, whose political allegiances were divided between two or more states, were also included, thereby confusing the traditional concept of national control. As a result the maintenance of internationally accepted frontiers with other Balkan states (and eastwards with Turkey) has led to serious military and diplomatic exchanges and many areas of tension remain.

The first territorial gains came in 1864 when Britain ceded the Ionian islands to Greece. Their acquisition was an immense gain, not only in wealth and population, but particularly in prestige, for Ionian society, unlike that of the Greek mainland, was highly stratified and its aristocratic culture, rooted in the centuries of Venetian rule and moulded in the principles of British statehood, proved beneficial to Athenian politics. Ionian agitation for union with Greece had developed by the 1860s into a powerful movement and Britain's reluctant decision to cede the islands was both a concession to Greek feelings and an unprecedented gesture of goodwill to the new King George I (formerly Prince William of Denmark) who had replaced Otho. The choice of a Danish prince was strongly influenced by Britain and the title 'King of the Hellenes', not 'King of Hellas', made it clear that his rule was to be the opposite to that of Otho. It was a tribute to George I that he was able, for nearly fifty years, to keep his footing in a system set up by the first democratic constitution of 1864. His long and important reign, during which Greece acquired most of its present boundaries, ended tragically with his assassination in 1913 by a Greek in the newly occupied city of Thessalonica.

Unlike the Ionian islands the province of Thessaly was no magnanimous gift; it was acquired in 1881 as the result of long negotiations by the protecting powers. In view of the language and religious affiliations of the province, the Greek claim was valid, but historically Thessaly had always acted as a forecourt to Greece from the north, and the stronger Turkish control of the province delayed its incorporation. In Berlin in June 1880 the Great Powers agreed on a frontier which favoured Greece for it included the Epirot districts of Ioannina and Metsoven. The Turks found this unacceptable and the Greeks retaliated with a threatening mobilisation of their armed forces – the first of many such confrontations which came to characterise Graeco-Turkish relationships. The question of Thessaly was reopened and a settlement reached in which the Turks agreed to forfeit the province together with the Arta region of Epirus; the cities and districts of Ioannina and Prevenza remained in Turkish hands.

The Greeks accepted these proposals with reluctance but they had, nonetheless, secured an important agricultural province and one destined to contribute notably to the national economy. Its capital, Larisa, for long a crossroads for communications between northern and central Greece, became an even more strategically important centre as the headquarters of the Greek First Army. With Thessaly Greece also gained the Aegean port of Volos situated at the head of the Pagastikos Gulf. It had degenerated into a squalid township of some 2,000 inhabitants but rapidly emerged as the maritime outlet for Thessalian cereals, cotton, tobacco and livestock, and as an important manufacturing town for textiles, tanning, olive-oil and cigarettes. Volos, in fact, rivalled the manufacturing potential of Piraeus until stricken by two disastrous earthquakes in 1945 and 1955.

CURRANTS AND SHIPS

The task of building a viable economy in a land where agriculture was backward and raw materials severely limited was one of major proportions. The Bavarian administration had totally disregarded the real needs and aspirations of the Greeks, particularly the peasant population which lived in a state of absolute misery entirely abandoned to their own fate. Good agricultural land was in short supply and the majority of the old Ottoman-owned estates passed, with independence, to the local Greek chiefs and notables or were bought outright by wealthy Greeks from Constantinople and other Turkish cities. Early legislation involving land redistribution was unco-ordinated and of limited success, but the legal recognition of squatters' rights was more effective and as late as 1961 an observer reported that 'a landlord must walk over his estate daily like a gamekeeper in order to protect it from squatters'.

Gradually agricultural land was brought back into cultivation though the character of farming changed little and followed what was essentially a subsistence regime. Its backwardness was a combination of many factors, not least the antiquated implements and techniques, and those areas fortunate enough to produce surplus crops were foiled in their attempts to market them by inadequate, often non-existent, transport facilities. It is reported that the coastal town of Nauplia and neighbouring Argos received grain supplies from as far away as Trieste and Alexandria, while the Tripolis region in the Arcadian mountains only 9km away had surplus supplies which were left to rot because of the lack of adequate roads. Only about 240km of road were built during Otho's reign and for large sections of the country wheeled traffic was an impossibility.

The basic problem in nineteenth-century Greek agriculture was how to produce some exportable product in sufficient quantities to pay for the necessary grain and other imports. The answer was found in dried currants and, subsequently, in tobacco – two intensive crops requiring much labour but comparatively little land. Under the Turks the northern

Peloponnesian coastal region produced currant grapes, called 'Corinthian', for the British market; despite the name the trade was centred on the port of Patras. With Greek independence new markets were developed in France, Italy, Austria and other continental countries and by 1878 the exportation of over 100,000 tons annually made the currant grape the cornerstone of the entire Greek economy. But the trade had been artificially stimulated by the phylloxera blight which drastically reduced the output of French vineyards. Greek production was increased to meet the demands of the French wine manufacturers who took approximately one-third of the total export. When phylloxera was brought under control and protective tarrifs introduced against Greek currants the trade, and farming in general, naturally suffered. Farmers turned to the production of Turkish or 'oriental' tobacco, but it was not until the resettlement and colonisation of Macedonia and Thrace that a large-scale tobacco trade became significant.

Greece's backward farming conditions were matched by its embryonic manufacturing sector. The handicraft industries of the Turkish period, especially textiles, suffered adversely from the competition of continental mass production and the only enterprises of note were the food-processing industries centred on Athens-Piraeus, Patras, Volos and Kalamata. The Trikoupis administration after 1882 led to a marked improvement in communications, and investment capital was attracted from Greek communities abroad, but the lack of skilled workers and an undeveloped urban proletariat meant that industry remained rudimentary.

Shipping, based on the traditions of the past, was the only industry in which nineteenth-century Greece had advantages and it proved to be a vital element in the economic growth of the country. Yet the advent of the steamship produced a crisis, for the Greek islanders, widely admired for their skills with sailing ships, had neither the funds nor the expertise for the new steam technology. Disaster was averted when wealthy Greeks from overseas began to purchase old steamships in Britain and elsewhere and lease them to Greek captains – those who have travelled on domestic shipping lines in the Aegean will know that this state of affairs continues! By 1895 the Greek merchant fleet had reached a total of 400,000 tons, of which 144,975 tons were steam, and goods were carried throughout the world.

Up until 1870 the Cyclades port of Syros, or Ermoupolis, was pre-eminent and the crossing-point of routes from the western Mediterranean to the Levant and from the Black Sea and the northern Aegean to Crete and Africa. Like Delos in antiquity, it was the centre of the entrepôt trade of many Aegean islands and its commerce mushroomed at the time of the War of Independence when it received many refugees fleeing from Turkish reprisals. The major factor in the decline of Ermoupolis was the opening in 1893 of the Corinth Canal linking the Gulf of Corinth with the Saronic Gulf. It attracted shipping between the Adriatic and the eastern Mediterranean and led to the rapid expansion of Piraeus as the centre of the country's coastal and international shipping. Ermoupolis, however, retained its ship-repairing industry and other trades and also its monopoly of 'Turkish Delight', an industry introduced by refugees from the mastic-producing island of Chios.

From ancient times the Greeks and Romans had thought of piercing the Corinthian isthmus to avoid the dangerous navigation of the southern Peloponnesus, and it was Nero who made the first genuine attempt to undertake the work. It was never completed and the slipways, over which small boats were hauled by slaves, are recorded as remaining in use until the eleventh century. A canal project was submitted by Virlet d'Aoust on the request of Capodistrias, but the present canal was begun by a French company in 1882 and completed by the Greeks. It is a straight cut 6,400 metres long, 24·6 metres wide and 8 metres deep, although the height of the cut is 40 metres above sea level. Subject to rock falls and having a strong current, which necessitates a cautious passage, the Corinth Canal is, nonetheless, heavily utilised, accommodating comparatively large vessels and shortening the distance from Piraeus to Brindisi by 320km. Ironically, the new city of Corinth, rebuilt on a new site after the earthquake of 1858, gained little from its canal. However, five years after its opening the population of Piraeus had increased to 34,327 and its harbour facilities, proving inadequate to serve the great influx of shipping, were improved and extended. The subsequent growth of the port has been directly linked with the expansion of the capital, and as in classical times Athens and Piraeus were to function as one economic and physical unit.

THE GREAT IDEA

Greek and Turkish animosity over territorial and boundary claims led to the complete mobilisation of their armed forces in 1897. The Great Powers were forced to intervene to save Greece from defeat and certain strategic points along the northern frontier of Thessaly were retroceded to Turkey. National pride was severely wounded and Greece's one thought was revenge. Opportunity soon came in the shape of an inter-Balkan alliance between Serbia, Bulgaria and Greece which ostensibly sought to defend Christian peoples in the Balkans against Turkish oppression. The Balkan Wars (1912–14) that followed proved disastrous to Turkey, already weakened by a war with Italy in North Africa. Greece's territorial gains, however, were considerable and the Great Idea came nearer to fulfilment when a young lawyer from Crete, Eleutherios Venizelos (1864–1936), made his dramatic entry into Greek political life.

The struggle for the union of Crete with Greece had taken on its own special characteristics. Numerous insurrections and periods of bloodshed had punctuated island life throughout the nineteenth century and the Cretan rallying cry, now immortalised as the title of one of Kazantzakis' regional novels, was 'Freedom and Death'. In 1898, following a period of compromise, inactivity, and rivalries, the Great Powers forced the Turks to leave and granted Crete autonomous status under a high commissioner, Prince George, younger son of George I. Though the Prince was warmly welcomed, many Cretans refused to settle for half measure and unrest again broke out, culminating with Venizelos leading an abortive revolution in 1905. Born at Mournies, now a suburb of Canea in western Crete, Venizelos was a staunch republican who had pledged himself to work for the union of his island with Greece. This took him to Athens in 1910 when he was elected as deputy and then as prime minister, a career whose *daimen* was the Great Idea.

Venizelos brought the Balkan Wars to a victorious climax and in the peace treaties that followed Greece increased its territory from 66,700 to just under 103,500sq km and its population from 2·6 million to 4·3 million. The whole of 'southern' Epirus now belonged to Greece, together with southern Macedonia, including the great city of Thessalonica. The liberation of Thessalonica by the Greek Crown Prince, soon to be King Constantine I, was indeed a great prize, but Greece also acquired the important cities of Ioannina and Kavala, the latter the centre of Macedonia's rich tobacco-growing lands. Crete was officially united with Greece and so were many of the islands of the eastern Aegean, except Imbros and Tenedos, which remained with Turkey, and the Dodecanese and Rhodes, which would have been included but for the fact that they had been occupied by Italy as a result of her war with Turkey two years earlier.

In spite of this long wished for territorial accomplishment some Greeks were still disappointed and the extended northern frontier from the Ionian Sea to the Nestos river in the east brought new military and border-control problems. Macedonia, for example, now subdivided between Greece, Albania, Yugoslavia and Bulgaria, was a region of ethnic complexity which led to conflicting national interests. From earliest times it had been a crossroads for migrating peoples and a pathway for trade and invasions, and was settled by Greeks, Bulgars, Serbs, Turks and Albanians, as well as by many minority groups including Jews, Vlachs and gypsies. On its liberation Thessalonica presented an ethnic microcosm of the northern province for only one-sixth of its 120,000 inhabitants were Greek; half, in fact, were Jews, next came the Turks, then smaller minorities of almost all the southern Balkan peoples.

Conflicting national interests presented acute difficulties in Epirus. In fact, Greece acquired only southern Epirus with the northern section remaining as southern Albania. Like Macedonia, the name Epirus was (and is) a regional designation for an area with some physical but no political or administrative unity and many Greeks regarded its Albanian section as *terra irredenta*. During World War I it was estimated that 40 per cent of the population of northern Epirus were Greek Orthodox and that at least one-sixth of its 320,000 inhabitants spoke Greek as their first language. These were obviously important figures for the Greek irredentist claims, but to complicate the picture it was also estimated that at least 100,000 Albanian-speaking peoples occupied northern Greece. Dispute over Epirus is the reason for the technical state of war which still exists between Albania and Greece and for the closed borders between the two countries.

The Treaty of Sèvres

Though Greece had not despatched a single soldier to fight the Turks in World War I, the peace treaty that followed it was highly favourable to the Greeks and enabled them, if only briefly, to fulfil most of their territorial desires for a Greater Greece. The Treaty of Sèvres (signed on 10 August 1920 but never ratified) was the abortive settlement forced on Ottoman Turkey which was obliged to renounce permanently its entire empire, including the European possessions, the Arab territories of Syria, Mesopotamia and Arabia and the territory of Armenia. Greece acquired Western and Eastern Thrace (up to Chatalja within 32km of Constantinople), the islands of Imbros and Tenedos and the city of Smyrna and its hinterland which was to come under a five-year administration, pending a plebiscite. The Greeks were prepared to keep the future of Constantinople open by making it an international city, but the internationalisation of the Straits (Dardanelles, Marmora and Bosporus) by allied forces, in which the Greeks were represented, assured the latter of sovereignty over Gallipoli and the entire western Asia Minor.

The Smyrna region was a vital Greek acquisition for it contained several hundred thousand Greeks and was seen as a refuge, in the case of oppression, for all Greeks in Asia Minor, of which there were at least 1·5 million. The city itself represented the authentic wealth of Asiatic Turkey for it was the empire's second largest manufacturing community, Anatolia's major trading outlet on the Mediterranean and the western terminus of the railway system. Under the terms of Sèvres, Turkish sovereignty in Smyrna was 'suspended' rather than abolished and it was stated that the Athens government would simply be responsible for the administration of the enclave. Turks living there would be treated as Greek nationals with their rights ostensibly protected by a minorities treaty signed by both Greece and the Allies.

For a time it seemed that the Greek dream would at last be realised, that the Greek empire would be reconstituted and that, with the final collapse of Turkey, liberated Constantinople would once more become the capital of Hellenism. This was not to be, for the triumph of Venizelos and his party was brief. The pro-German sympathies of King Constantine during World War I had led Venizelos to set up a separate national government at Thessalonica. In 1917 the King was forced to abdicate in favour of his son Alexander, whose accidental death in 1920 posed a problem of succession. Constantine was recalled but the internal schisms – the bane of Greek politics – between monarchists and republicans weakened the country and with the switch of interests on the part of the Allies, Greece was left almost alone with the problem of enforcing the Treaty of Sèvres. In Turkey Mustapha Kemal, the future Ataturk, had begun to reorganise the national forces and the Greek move to launch a general offensive against the republican movement in Ankara ended in disaster. In August 1922 the Greek army was smashed and fled in disorder before the Turks, who pursued its remnants into the sea, slaughtering thousands and burning Smyrna. This marked the end of 2,500 years of Greek supremacy in western Anatolia and the collapse of the Great Idea. The Smyrna disaster was to have a profound and lasting effect on Greek life for Turkey under the Kemalists demanded a new settlement.

The Greek handicraft industry has greatly benefited from the country's rapid expansion in tourism. Throughout Greece crafts such as textiles, pottery and ceramics, lace, carpets and woodwork increasingly cater for the gift and souvenir market (*Lower photograph**)

The Argo-Saronic island of Hydra played a major sea-faring role in the Greek War of Independence. Large villas dominate its small, enclosed harbour and bear witness to its former prosperity*

The Treaty of Lausanne

The settlement came in 1923 with the Treaty of Lausanne, which, with minor exceptions was to draw the final frontiers of Greece. The only subsequent territorial adjustment was the addition of the Dodecanese islands which were ceded to Greece by the Italians in 1947. Under the terms of Lausanne Greece lost Eastern Thrace, the islands of Imbros and Tenedos, Smyrna and the Anatolian provinces. But of far greater significance in human terms was the clause in the Lausanne treaty dealing with the fate of the Greek and other ethnic groups in Turkey. The initiative had come from Venizelos, and the Allies endorsed the plea that the minorities be protected with written guarantees under League of Nations supervision. The Turkish government rejected this view claiming, among other things, that the issue was academic since the flight of the Greeks was already taking place. This, treated as a *fait accompli*, was made the political basis for a mutual exchange of Greek and Turkish populations. Venizelos insisted that the well-integrated Greek population of Constantinople should be allowed to remain and that the Greek Patriarch should similarly be permitted to maintain his seat in the old Byzantine capital. Reluctantly the Turks agreed, though initially they regarded even the Patriarch himself as an 'exchangeable Greek'. As it happened a large proportion of Greeks left Constantinople for Greece.

A mixed committee was set up to supervise the exchanges and to ensure that the Turks returning to Turkey would receive property equal in value to the property they had abandoned in Greece. The same terms were applied to the Greeks. When the agreement was signed the irredentist question that had plagued the Ottoman empire for centuries was laid to rest and the exchange represented the most daring and unprecedented solution to an endemic political problem ever to have been devised in modern history. Similar arrangements were undertaken for the transference of Bulgarians and Greeks between their respective countries. Some 93,000 Bulgarians had previously resided in Greece and the Turks had numbered around 450,000. In sheer physical terms Greece took the brunt of the problem, receiving from Turkey alone over 1·2 million refugees which in 1923 was equivalent to 22 per cent of the country's population.

The arrival of the refugees (eventually destined to become a new and vital factor in the economic and social fabric) confronted Greece, already bankrupt and demoralised, with tremendous resettlement problems. Most of them were totally without resources and many thousands, including a fair proportion of widows and children, were forced to the large towns such as Athens, Piraeus and Thessalonica to live in shanty settlements of appalling conditions. The population of Athens increased from 292,991 in 1920 to 459,211 in 1928, of which 129,380 were refugees. The corresponding increase in Piraeus was from 133,482 to 259,659, with a refugee total of 101,185. Under the pressure of circumstances they were encouraged to build illegally and large shanty townships without any provision for amenities and sanitation grew up around the country's main urban centres. In Athens and elsewhere many of these townships (now redeveloped as attractive residential districts) were nostalgically christened with names such as New Ionia and New Smyrna.

Away from the cities the refugees took over the lands vacated by the Turks and other minority groups and enormous international help was given for their care and resettlement, especially in the newly acquired northern provinces of Macedonia and Thrace. Here refugees comprised 45 per cent and 35 per cent respectively of the population, whereas the Peloponnesus, for example, housed a mere 2·7 per cent. Land was alloted to families or to groups and gradually extensive areas were reclaimed and brought back into profitable cultivation. In 1929, Sir John Campbell, vice-chairman of the resettlement committee, summed up the results of the work in northern Greece: 'The aspect of the country has entirely changed. Everywhere one sees the cheerful red roofs of the colonisation settlers. Where formerly vast uncultivated plains stretched, there are now flourishing villages full of life, and showing obvious signs of comfort and in many cases prosperity.' Certainly the agricultural statistics bore out Sir John's observations for Macedonia and Thrace became important producers of cereals, vegetables and tobacco which proved to be of great benefit to both the domestic and the foreign market.

For Greece the interwar period was one of grave economic and social problems, but at the same time it was a period of great transformation for many of the Asia Minor refugees brought commercial expertise, and skills in industry as well as in agriculture. Politically, however, the country was greatly disturbed. The humiliating defeat by Turkey had forced Constantine into exile for the second time (1922) and he died a few months later. There then followed a dispute between the republicans and royalists during which George II, Constantine's successor, left Greece without officially abdicating. On 25 March 1924 a republic was proclaimed, but between that date and 1928 Greece suffered 10 prime ministers, 3 general elections and 11 military coups. Venizelos failed to establish anything like moderation in Greek politics during this period and died in exile in Paris in 1936. One year earlier the monarchy had been precariously restored with the return of George II, but a new political rot was spreading across Europe and into Greece – Fascism. When General John Metaxas seized control of Athens in 1936 he began modelling it along Axis lines, operating a police state with detention camps, torture and rigid censorship. The country was to experience a similarly brutal regime in the 1960s and early 1970s.

8

National Games and Daily Bread

The modern Greeks have been described as the most politically obsessed people on earth, with the result that political life since the establishment of the state has been both intensely active and highly unstable. The periods of democracy, dictatorship, oligarchy, tyranny, 'crown democracy' and republic, the number and variety of political parties, the constant change in their dramatis personae, and the short average life of governments, collectively reveal the political involvement of the Greeks which amounts to a national pastime. As one author recently put it, 'politics not Euripides is the national drama and one which entails not merely the frequent changing of cast but also the play.' Unlike many western countries where political parties are highly organised, semi-permanent groups with an elected head, in Greece they appear, disappear and reappear in constant succession and tend to be formed by and to reflect the opinions of their leaders. When a leader falls out of favour, as frequently happens, the party also disintegrates or reforms under a new title or political doctrine. Some of the country's main political events prior to its involvement in World War II were briefly outlined in the previous chapter. Since the war Greece has continued to be torn by its political immaturity and has experienced well over forty government changes in something like thirty-five years. Added to this the country has suffered a highly destructive civil war and an oppressive and demoralising military junta; the Greek monarchy has again been overthrown and replaced by a republican system, and the country has adversely suffered from Greek-Turkish antagonism, arising from a mixture of pressing political issues and deep-rooted prejudices.

The instability of Greek politics has often been related to the volatile, hot-headed and highly individualistic temperament of its people, whose political factions, it is said, fight each other with the fierce ardour of the wars of the city states. Yet this internal strife is also a reflection of the country's external politics regarding its strategic importance in south-east Europe. Since independence its sovereignty has been subject to the veto of whatever greater power looms over the eastern Mediterranean, whether it be Britain, Germany, the United States or, in the case of the more recent Cyprus troubles, Turkey. Greece today occupies a position in an otherwise communist-geared Balkans and is fully conscious of its tactical vulnerability. Its northern frontiers border Albania, Yugoslavia and Bulgaria for 990km, and at the nearest point the Bulgarian border is only 24km from the Aegean coast. It was natural, therefore, that Greece should be attracted by the security system offered by NATO and a combination of events in 1968, including the Russian threats against Yugoslavia and Albania, strengthened these ties with the establishment of a joint naval force in the eastern Mediterranean in which Greece supplied the ships when necessary. The country's position in NATO, and particularly its relationship with the United States, has wavered during the last decade, and in view of this it is not difficult to appreciate Greece's attachment to entry into the EEC. This must be seen as another bid for economic and moral support from the Western world, Greece's recognition, in fact, of its own vulnerability in world affairs.

WAR AND CIVIL WAR

The Greeks believe that their country has been a primary Russian objective for a long time and view their civil war, which tore the country apart just over thirty years ago, as an attempt by the Soviet Union to bring Greece within its orbit. The seeds of communism were sown during World War II when Greece's direct involvement in 1940 came as a result of Mussolini's threats from occupied Albania, where no fewer than 125,000 Italian troops were concentrated. On 28 October the Italian minister in Athens presented an ultimatum to General

Metaxas demanding the cession of Ioannina and the Epirus coast to Albania, which technically meant to Italy. Through Metaxas' defiant 'no' ('*ochi*') to Mussolini's pressures, Britain, facing the Axis powers alone, gained her only fighting ally outside the empire. Mussolini's troops had expected little resistance, but all Italian counter-offensives were beaten back in what was virtually a spontaneous uprising by the Greeks. This was Metaxas' finest hour and 'Ochi Day' is still celebrated as a Greek national holiday, second only to Independence Day.

By 1941 the German timetable had caught up with Greece, forcing George II and his government into exile and Metaxas to commit suicide. In little more than three months their Greek campaign was almost over and many of the 58,000 British and Imperial forces then in Greece were forced to take refuge in Crete where, with local support, they made a bold stand. But on 20 May the island witnessed a spectacular invasion by German paratroopers and, once Maleme airport, west of Canea, was taken, reinforcements poured in. By 30 May the battle of Crete was over and thousands of British troops escaped across the mountains to the south coast from whence they were conveyed to Egypt. The imposing eagle, off the main road three miles west of Canea, is the German memorial to their parachute assault, but it is interesting that after the war it was revealed that the German High Command regarded the airborne operation as something of a disaster, in view of its heavy casualty rate. The Cretans have chosen to leave the eagle as a memorial to their own valour in the operations.

Greece under Axis occupation again became a fragmented country divided among conquering powers with the Ionian islands officially annexed by Italy, eastern Macedonia and Thrace by Bulgaria and the rest of the country divided into German, Italian and Bulgarian occupation zones. The Germans occupied Athens, Thessalonica and Crete and under them Greece suffered extreme hardships. The country was sucked dry of food and resources and famines led to countless deaths, particularly among children and the aged. It is estimated that almost 300,000 people died in the winter of 1941–2 when every morning trucks and carts collected the corpses of those fallen victim to starvation and cold. In Thessalonica the 60,000 strong Jewish population was rounded up for despatch to Poland and subsequent extermination and it is recorded that only 6,000 survived, principally those who had taken to the mountains.

Deprivations of all kinds and punitive retaliations against villages were particularly common on Crete where, as elsewhere in Greece, widespread resistance had developed in the form of guerrilla and partisan movements, aided by special British agents. As in Turkish times their leaders were desperadoes of one kind or another (usually ex-army officers of the middle rank) and their main preoccupation, after keeping alive, was the harassment of the enemy. The National Liberation Front (EAM) was undoubtedly the strongest of these resistance movements and, initially aided by Britain, it fully expected an imminent liberation of Greece by the Allies. In reality it was a front for communism and it lost its British support in 1943 when Britain became concerned about what would happen to Greece when the Axis powers were defeated. Military support shifted to the National Republican Greek League (EDES) which represented the less radical views of the exiled government, but ultimately it fell to Britain to resolve the disputes and ideological clashes between these two factions. The bitterness was more than Britain could handle, for the evils of the Axis occupation were now compounded by the greater evils of an underground civil war. With the liberation of Greece in 1944 and the end of the hostilities in Europe in the spring of 1945, Russia, which hitherto had tacitly approved the British efforts in Greece, now decided to intervene on the side of EAM.

Thus the 1944–9 period was one of continual bloodshed and terrorism in Greece for the country, in reality, was the battleground for Eastern and Western ideologies. 'The communist inspired war in Greece', states Kenneth Young (*The Greek Passion*), 'was the first all out example of war in which Russia and the West were the puppet-masters and the puppets the Greeks, as later Koreans and Vietnamese' and, it might be added, Cambodians. The 1946 plebiscite which brought back King George II did nothing to halt hostilities and Britain, preoccupied with troubles at home, appealed to the United States in a bid to save Greece from becoming a communist satellite. A United States economic mission was despatched and temporarily given a major role in the EDES government, and a military mission aided the reorganisation of the regular Greek army that had come into being. Terror, reprisals and counter-reprisals grew in intensity, but American pressure succeeded in squashing Russian support and the final defeat of the communist forces by Field-Marshal Papagos and the National Army came in 1949. George II had died two years earlier and his brother Paul succeeded him to the throne. To strengthen links with the West, Greece was admitted to NATO in 1952.

The civil war had devastated Greece. According to official figures the cost was 40,000 lives, but unofficial estimates range as high as 158,000 and the number made homeless was incalculable, for hundreds of settlements were destroyed. Another 80,000–100,000 people crossed the borders as refugees and were absorbed in various communist countries, the largest colony being at Tashkent in Central Asia. Mines and factories were also destroyed, agricultural land abandoned, and road, rail and port facilities completely disrupted. Not surprisingly, memories of the Greek civil war are an ever-present background to the country's politics today.

RECONSTRUCTION AND REVOLUTION

Following the civil war, the 1952 elections gave power to Marshal Papagos, the leader of the National Union party which, not unexpectedly, was of the extreme right. He continued as prime minister until 1955 when the leadership passed to Constantine Karamanlis whose four terms in office up to 1963 marked the longest period of uninterrupted government in modern Greek history. As a leader Karamanlis showed surprising magnetism at the polls and velvet-glove firmness in office. Internationally, the major thorn in his political side was the Cyprus issue; demonstrations for and against its union with Greece rapidly multiplied, culminating in extreme antagonism and open violence on Cypriot soil between Briton and Greek. But in February 1959, in what seemed like a miracle, the Greek, Turkish and British representatives, at a meeting in London, recognised the island's independence, with Britain preserving its strategic naval bases and the Turkish minority their national rights. Cypriot independence rocked the Karamanlis administration, for many Greeks, still regarding the island as irredentist territory, felt that he had underplayed the issue. His resignation and self-imposed exile in Paris, however, was related more to his grievances with the Greek royal family and to a series of political scandals than to his questionable misrepresentation of Cyprus.

The Greek premiership now passed to George Papandreou, leader of the Centre Union Party. He attempted the difficult task of balancing the left against the right in Greek politics and, inevitably, his term in office began yet another stormy period in the country's political life. The sense of economic and political security built up by Karamanlis disintegrated into turmoil, with episodes of mob violence, and Papandreou was ousted in July 1965, almost a year after the death of King Paul and the accession of his son Constantine II. Many have regarded the fall of Papandreou and his liberalisation policies as one of the most tragic events in post-war Greek politics and there is now considerable support for the view that his fall was engineered by the American government or its agencies, thus encouraging the eventual military takeover. A succession of short-lived governments followed Papandreou and from December 1966 a non-political administration held office charged with the organisation of a general election. This event was forestalled by the bloodless, but subsequently infamous, coup d'état of April 1967.

The Generals
The April revolution revealed to the world at large both the internal and external political weaknesses of Greece. Initially it was reported to have stemmed from a clash between the right-wing monarchists and militia and the communist-biased

leftists who threatened to undermine constitutional monarchy. But the junta's claim that it had moved to thwart a communist takeover was soon recognised to be an insignificant factor in the coup and a scapegoat argument. In the thirty-two years since the Metaxas dictatorship Greek politics had been firmly in the hands of the palace and its right-wing supporters. Despite the political volatility this control never wavered and had never been seriously challenged until Papandreou's attempt to break down the traditional distribution of power. There is strong evidence that the coup was engineered to prevent the victory of the Centre Union at the polls. The supposed innocence of King Constantine is now heavily discredited, but an abortive attempt was made by him to overthrow the regime which, in traditional Greek monarchical style, culminated in his self-imposed exile in Rome on 13 December 1967.

In the beginning it was important that the officers who planned the coup (on present evidence they numbered no more than forty) should gain Constantine's approval and, hence, some kind of legality. They were forced, therefore, to submit to the King's insistence that the majority of the cabinet should be made up of civilians. Thus a triumvirate of relatively junior army officers were the only plotters to take ministerial office. The senior, a tank brigadier, Stylianos Pattakos, became minister of the interior; a colonel from the intelligence, Nicholas Makarezos, took over the nation's economic affairs; and an artillery colonel, George Papadopoulos, installed himself in the key post of minister of the prime minister's office. It was soon clear that Papadopoulos was the man who really mattered especially after Constantine's counter-coup when he had himself sworn in as prime minister and minister of national defence.

The junta's propaganda was rapid and the slogans, symbols and placards of the Generals' Greece were placed at strategic points throughout the country – along the main highways, at the approach to harbours, at airport terminals and at the entrance to every town, village and hamlet. Its emblem was a phoenix arising out of flames behind the silhouette of an armed soldier and carried the words '21 April, 1967' and 'Greece'. Its message was plain: on the day of the revolution a new Greece was born which would rise to glory under the protection of the armed forces. Yet the generals had no clear ideas of the sort of regime they wished to establish and, lacking any popular support, they began to consolidate their position in a series of edicts which the army was quick to direct to the civilian public. Repression began in true comic opera style when a ban was imposed on beards and long hair for men and on mini-skirts for women, tourists included. But army orders reached graver proportions in press censorship and in the control of the education system and all mass media. The freedom of the individual was further abused in the large-scale arrests that accompanied the junta's rise to power and the reports of torture, later to be confirmed, led to anti-junta campaigns throughout the Western world. In April 1970, the release of over 300 political prisoners, including the popular composer Theodorakis, indicated some relaxation in the junta's detention policy, though the police society with its torture methods persisted.

The colonels' regime was far from stable and repressive methods were necessary to maintain its precarious existence. On 1 June 1973, following allegations of a plot within the navy to overthrow the government, the monarchy was abolished and a republic established under the presidency of Papadopoulos. A referendum (of dubious honesty) confirmed the new presidential constitution and a civilian government was appointed, headed by Markezinis. The heroic student revolt in November 1973 was instrumental in bringing down the Papadopoulos administration. Known as the siege of the Athens Polytechnic, it won great admiration and sympathy throughout the world, though there were many civilian casualties and a period of martial law was enforced. Papadopoulos was ousted by a conservative military group under the leadership of General Dimitrios Ioannides whose government was equally repressive. His regime's greatest political and tactical miscalculation was the engineering of the Cyprus coup in July 1974, which deposed its president, Archbishop Makarios. Led by the Greek officers of the Cypriot

National Guard, it caused an international crisis of major importance leading to the Turkish invasion of the island and its consequent military partition. Finding the chain of events too difficult to handle and with the voice of the world against them, the junta, on 23 July, relinquished its power.

Karamanlis, patiently waiting in Paris, was called from his exile to administer the chaos that the generals had left behind. Their seven-year regime, though it started soundly in the material sense, had subsequently undermined the very bases of the country. Economic and political sanctions had been instrumental in Greece's withdrawal from the Council of Europe and aid from the EEC to the junta government had been temporarily frozen. The Cyprus issue had also precipitated the Greek withdrawal from the military arm of NATO. On 17 November 1974, Greece held its first general elections in ten years and Karamanlis' New Democracy Party polled 54·3 per cent of the vote and gained 220 out of the 300 parliamentary seats (though this was subsequently reduced in by-elections). The constitutional power of the King remained unsettled until 8 December when a referendum rejected 'crown democracy' and, therefore the return of Constantine, in favour of a republic. Under the new constitution of January 1975, Constantine Tsatses became President of the Hellenic Republic, assuming his office in June of that year.

The major domestic problem facing Greece today is that of getting its house in order following the period of military rule. The return of civilian government has brought a renewal of co-operation with Western Europe, particularly its political and economic association with the EEC which promises Greece full membership in 1981. In terms of foreign policy, however, the most contentious problem, as earlier this century, concerns its relationship with Turkey and relates to boundary questions in the Aegean Sea, made all the more pressing since the discovery of what may be commercially significant oil reserves south of the island of Thasos. Geographically the Aegean basin unites Greece and Turkey, but politically it divides them. The Greeks have always regarded the Aegean as their sea and now invoke the Geneva Convention of 1959 which specifies that all islands are entitled to a continental shelf. Many of the Greek islands, however, lie within a few kilometres of the Anatolian coast and the Turkish argument is that they 'rest' on the Turkish continental shelf. Turkey has drawn an imaginary median line through the Aegean and has issued oil drilling licences in its eastern half, even to the west of the Greek islands of Lesbos, Chios and Lemnos. Thus like Santorini of old, the Aegean volcano may explode the moment the Greeks or the Turks attempt to permanently extend their territorial waters.

THE REGIONAL PROBLEM

Though Greece can no longer be considered as an undeveloped country there are obvious differences in per capita incomes and other indices of economic status between Greece and the EEC with which it is now associated. Its gross domestic product is still one of the lowest in Europe but its percentage growth of 5·2 over the 1970–6 period is particularly impressive and is reflected in most sectors of the economy. Measures to modernise agriculture, to promote industrialisation and to place both on a competitive basis are numerous and complex, and corresponding developments in communications and energy production have similarly made substantial progress. Tourism, shipping and remittances from Greek workers abroad are the country's greatest earners of foreign exchange and this important inflow of capital is vital to the country's balance of payment deficit. In recent years, too, Greece's proximity to the Middle East has been advantageous. Many of the offices which were destroyed or forced out of battle-torn Beirut moved to Athens and Piraeus, providing not only construction and office employment but again valuable foreign exchange. Also, Greek businessmen, traditionally always on good terms with Arab buyers, have moved, often with considerable workforces, into the oil-rich capitals.

Greece now boasts a mixed economy, but it is one with a large agricultural sector, absorbing 35 per cent of the labour force and contributing to only 15 per cent of the gross domestic product. In spite of widespread changes and revolutionary improvements agriculture has lagged far behind the growth rate of manufacturing industry and, for that matter, tourism, with the result that marked inequalities in incomes and general standards of living occur between the rural and non-rural branches of the economy. Agricultural per capita incomes average about 36 per cent of the corresponding incomes in the manufacturing sector and about 52 per cent of the national average.

Adding to the problem of occupational inequality is the fact that industry and commerce show an overwhelming concentration in the Athens-Piraeus area which, as the national capital, provides important locational advantages, not least the presence of a large metropolitan market. According to 1976 estimates the population of Greater Athens (which includes Piraeus and numerous satellite towns) was over 2·5 million (or 28 per cent of the country's 9·1 million inhabitants) and it accounted for 52 per cent of the total number of industrial and manufacturing establishments and 55 per cent of the total workforce employed in industry. In terms of its size and commercial importance, Thessalonica, with a population of over 557,000, is an important magnet for northern Greece but fails to compete with the pull of Athens, and Greece's other cities tend to be much smaller and provincial in character; for example, Patras has a population of around 120,000, Volos 88,000, Iraklion 85,000 and Larisa 73,000; only three other centres have populations above 40,000.

The development problem in Greece, therefore, is twofold: not only is there a marked and growing disparity in income levels between rural and urban areas, there are also significant inequalities between the capital area and the rest of the country. Stated more bluntly the problem is that of an economically advanced Athens versus the regions, which a recent OECD report called 'lagging and backward'. Having gained a lead over other centres, a process of cumulative expansion has occurred in Athens as political and economic progress and social advances are concentrated there. The city is the seat of a highly centralised government and the home of its ruling families and intelligentsia and, not surprisingly, it has been favoured with a higher proportion of national spending. The capital has more doctors, hospital beds, dentists, teachers and professional people per head of population than anywhere else in Greece and its social life is by far the most developed that the country can offer. In domestic facilities, the high proportion of houses in the capital which have baths or showers, televisions and telephones stands in marked contrast to the provinces, as does the difference in the per capita consumption of electric energy.

The Migrant Greek

The Greek regional problem has led to an important internal redistribution of population, from rural areas to the towns and cities, particularly to Athens and to a lesser extent Thessalonica. Migration is a pervasive feature of Greek history and it has often been argued that, as with the Irish, it is a response to more or less ephemeral psychological impulses. Certainly emigration has long had its place in Greek tradition and throughout this century it has been advanced as one solution to the country's economic problems. Before World War II the United States was the main destination, but subsequently its place was taken by Canada and Australia. Then came the great labour shortages in Belgian and West German heavy industry which attracted thousands of Greeks as transient workers; in 1976 something like 290,000 Greeks were working abroad in the EEC countries – 125,000 in West Germany and 50,000 in Britain. In spite of acute psycho-sociological problems at both the local and national levels, emigration has a compensating effect on the Greek economy. Not only has it lessened the problems of unemployment, it has also substantially strengthened the country's balance of payments. Between January and July 1976, for example, remittances from workers abroad amounted to $425 million but such trends are changing as opportunities diminish in the West and the country's own economy develops.

The search for job opportunities is also behind the present high rate of internal migration and statistics have shown that since 1951 the rate of population increase in Greater Athens and in the country's other principal cities substantially exceeded the overall national increase, reflecting the high level of rural-urban movement. Since this date the population of Athens has increased by over 35 per cent, Thessalonica by 29 per cent, Larisa by 26 per cent and Iraklion by 22 per cent. As in other countries where migration is a natural feature, it is the younger element that shows the greatest propensity to leave with the result that the population of provincial areas is ageing. It is estimated that there are at least 300,000 deserted farms and houses in Greece, the majority of them in remote or sparsely populated areas.

The Problem City

The continual and rapid physical expansion of Athens has posed severe problems for the urban planners. Today, like most large conurbations, it suffers from the full range of urban diseases, including intense overcrowding, shortage of inner city building land, imminent traffic paralysis, noise and atmospheric pollution. As was the case earlier this century, when it faced the settlement problem of Asia Minor refugees, the city's modern housing problem is one of keeping pace with rapid population increase. Housing in Greece is based on the private market and since 1960 the average number of building permits granted in Athens has risen by 10 per cent annually. Numerous dwellings, often in good condition, have been demolished in order to provide the more profitable multi-rise apartment blocks which are the distinctive feature of the cityscape. Athenian apartments are usually between four and seven storeys in height. Most have balconies, and the top storeys on higher blocks are stepped back in order to conform to daylight regulations. Flat roofs may have penthouses or roof gardens and these create an often colourful, if jumbled, view, latticed with aerials, washing, plants and pollution-control devices. High density blocks, therefore, are common throughout the urban area, even on its edges where illegal housing districts (illegal in the sense that no planning permission has been given) continue to mushroom. In time these urban adjuncts, constructed by or for immigrant families,

A side alley in Myconos. Cubic houses of rough stone, plastered over and then whitewashed are characteristic of the Cyclades islands*

Though not the traditional view of the Greek environment, snow is not uncommon in exposed mountainous regions and on Mount Parnassus ski-ing is now a popular winter pastime.

are included on the city map, though this is no guarantee that they will be given the necessary urban services and amenities. Athens as well as Thessalonica, Iraklion and other centres have large peripheral shanty districts where the inhabitants live, in many cases, in conditions of extreme squalor and poverty, though rarely is this reflected in the personal hygiene of the inhabitants.

High residential density contributes to the already overloaded Athenian transport system and to general traffic congestion, the metropolitan area having over half of all the registered vehicles in Greece. An underground system to relieve such pressure is in its early stages of construction and will augment the existing (and partly underground) electric railway linking Piraeus with Kifissia via central Athens. Apart from this system and the two mainline stations, Athens has no real rail network, though the city is crossed by trolley-bus routes and a dense network of bus lines links all districts and suburbs with the centre.

The reorganisation of Athens is constantly under discussion and it seems that only a bold policy of decentralisation will ease its difficulties and benefit Greece as a whole. Proposals for the creation of new towns within a radius of thirty miles of central Athens, and suggestions to resite its international airport and to move the government and administrative quarters out of the city, are all seen as answers to over-centralisation. The problem is acute, for Athens, as the country's principal pole of attraction, continues to grow, largely at the expense of the rest of the country.

AGRICULTURE

The problems involved in placing Greek agriculture on a competitive basis, in the hope of stemming the tide of rural-urban migration, are immeasurable. Of the country's total agricultural area only 28 per cent is officially classified as arable land and even here the definition includes much land of low quality, as well as land in fallow and, hence, uncultivated for up to four or five years. Slope and altitude greatly restrict cultivation, and farming in many areas has extended beyond the limits consistent with conservational land use. Even in Macedonia and Thessaly the extensive reclamation projects of this century have virtually exhausted the limits of further cultivation. Elsewhere the most productive land occurs in a series of discontinuous coastal plains or in higher interior plains in mountainous districts.

Climatic influences are also restrictive, and one of the major difficulties is water shortage, especially during the summer when rainfall totals are low and evaporation rates high. Rainfall amounts are irregular from year to year, and large areas of limestone and porous subsoils hinder the construction of storage dams. Only 15 per cent of the land under cultivation is irrigated though official estimates indicate that the water potential of the country, if properly managed, is sufficient for the irrigation of 45 per cent of the present cultivated area.

Another factor limiting agriculture is the poor and for the most part exhausted soil which is the product of centuries of misuse and mismanagement. Soil erosion is widespread and Plato's description of the soils of Attica as 'the bones of a body wasted with disease' applies to large sections of the country today. One of the main causes of soil erosion is overstocking, particularly with goats, of which there are over 3 million, and the problem is compounded by the presence of a further 6 million sheep.

Greece, therefore, has some of the poorest agricultural land per capita in Europe and the resultant rural pressure on available farmland is further intensified by the still prevalent inheritance laws which lead to the subdivision of farmed areas into small, privately owned holdings consisting of a number of scattered plots. Fragmentation is greatest in Crete where each farmer has an average of thirteen plots per holding and it has been estimated that the average walking time for a Cretan farmer is ten minutes to his nearest plots and ninety minutes to his farthest. This, together with the low level of technology, is a principal factor in causing low productivity, both in yields per acre and in per worker employed. Farm fragmentation also mitigates against mechanisation and other improvements.

Through legislation and persuasion, contemporary governments have attempted to discourage those factors which contribute to fragmentation, that is, dowry and land inheritance laws, both of which stem from Byzantine and Turkish times.

Greek cultivation is still predominantly concerned with tilled field crops such as wheat, tobacco and cotton. Vine-growing, although more limited than in the past, is traditional and in some regions is the sole undertaking. In the Peloponnesus and Crete, Corinthian currants and sultana raisins, respectively, provide the main source of income for a large proportion of the rural population. However, in recent years the cultivation of citrus and other fruits has expanded and these have tended to replace vines as a major source of income. The olive is also a traditional crop with its harvest greatly influencing total annual agricultural incomes.

A permanent problem confronting agricultural policy is the tenacity with which the farming community persists with some traditional crops such as wheat and tobacco; for many years the wheat crop has exceeded domestic requirements, and although large amounts are exported the government has had to purchase the surplus at artificially high prices thereby throwing a heavy and unnecessary burden on the national budget. Tobacco production presents a similar problem with over-production creating disposal difficulties in a world market congested with tobacco of the oriental type. Through incentives and subsidies agricultural policy has been directed to inducing farmers to turn part of their lands over to other enterprises such as cotton, citrus fruits and fodder crops. The latter, in relation to the country's livestock sector, has been the object of a number of studies and meat production has expanded substantially since the 1960s. Encouragement has been given to commercial-sized production units to take the place of the traditional small farms and large areas of under-used land have been improved for grazing purposes. The tourist industry has greatly increased the demand for animal products, but Greece still spends something like $100 million annually on meat and dairy imports.

Greece regards its agricultural sector as complementary to rather than competitive with that of the EEC. It has obvious natural production advantages in crops such as currants, tobacco, olives, early vegetables and citrus and other fruits, whereas the EEC has an advantage, for example, in dairy produce. It is hoped that full membership will stabilise agricultural prices and encourage the restructuring of the crop system, the further setting up of agricultural co-operatives and the more extensive use of mechanisation. Wider markets, combined with the introduction of modern management techniques, might well revolutionise Greek agriculture.

Forestry and Fisheries

Centuries of burning, over-grazing by the goat and general mismanagement have stripped Greece of much of its original vegetation cover. Roughly 18 per cent of the country is classified as having some kind of forest cover but at least one-quarter of this consists of the secondary and stunted *maquis*-type growth which is of little commercial value. Reafforestation is taking place and today Macedonia accounts for over 30 per cent of forestry output, though forestry products represent only 3.2 per cent of primary production. Building timber fails to meet domestic requirements and the production of resin greatly fluctuates with changes in demand and price.

Fishing is a traditional Greek activity, but the number of inhabitants making a living from it is estimated at only 52,000 and income from this industry represents less than 1 per cent of gross domestic product. The government has constructed special quays and refrigeration units at principal fishing ports in an attempt to organise the industry more effectively, but over-fishing in the Mediterranean and its ever-increasing level of pollution are detrimental. Greek boats, however, fish Atlantic waters. Sponge fishing, formerly a major activity of Greek islanders, has also witnessed a dramatic decline, the culprit here being the manufacture of the synthetic product.

MINERALS AND MANUFACTURING

Minerals have played a significant role in Greece's economic progress and today resources of ferro-nickel, asbestos, magnesium, bauxite and iron ore provide the basis for such industries as petrochemicals and various branches of metallurgy. Greece has large proven deposits of lignite at Aliverion and Ptolemais in Western Macedonia and at Megalopolis in the central Peloponnesus and it is hoped that in the next few years the amount of electricity generated from lignite will rise from the present one-third to around two-thirds. Electrical energy from large thermal power plants and the significant, but more limited, hydro-electric projects, now provides an expanding basis for industrialisation and for the rise of social standards throughout Greece. Initial optimism over the discovery of oil and natural gas in the Aegean and Ionian Seas has not yet been justified, but the latest appraisal confirms the original estimate of 25,000 barrels a day, or about 1,250,000 metric tons of crude oil a year, which at current prices is worth over $100 million. But it will require an investment of $250 million in production platforms, submarine pipelines and offshore installations to exploit the oil, and according to the Ministry of Industry, all indications show the Aegean sea bed to be fragmented by innumerable faults making exploitation difficult, if not commercially unsound. The latest estimates of gas reserves suggest that they will run dry within twenty years.

One of the most important steps in the development of Greek heavy industry was the establishment of Aluminium of Greece in 1960, a joint undertaking by Pechiney of France and the Greek Development Organisation. Situated at Aspra Spitia on the northern coast of the Gulf of Corinth, it is now the largest corporate enterprise in Greece, both in terms of assets owned and in income generated. But the largest manufactured item for export in 1976 was nickel, produced by the Greek company Larco S A whose rapid expansion is one of the country's major success stories. Another complex which has greatly changed the picture of Greek industrial production is the Esso-Pappas group of companies whose base is the oil refinery at Thessalonica which succeeded the state refinery set up at Aspropyrgos, near Athens, in 1959. An ammonia plant, the North Greek Chemicals and the Hellenic Steel Company are integral parts of the industrial complex at Thessalonica. The future shape of the Greek steel industry, especially that of the Halivourghiki mills, near Athens, depends on another important industry, shipbuilding, of which the country's largest yard is the Hellenic Shipyards at Skaramanga, though other yards for building, repairing and refitting ships occupy the Bay of Eleusis to the west of Athens.

Perhaps one of the most promising sectors of the Greek manufacturing scene is the textile industry. Greece is the only European country to produce its own cotton and great efforts are now being made to expand the present output which stands at around 100,000 tons. The manufacturing of cotton fabrics is still in its early stages but there are already indications that firms in Europe are looking to Greeçe as a base for subsidiary operations. Piraiki-Patraiki is the country's largest firm, producing something like 12,000 tons of cotton yarn annually of which 4,500 tons are exported. Similarly, the Greek electronics industry sees its future expansion tied to co-operation with large EEC firms. In general, labour shortages, high wage rates and strikes are encouraging EEC firms to look elsewhere for suppliers and Greek businessmen believe that many doors may soon be open to them.

TOURISM

Long, hot summers, relatively mild winters, a varied and beautiful countryside, some of the world's most famous archaeological and historical sites, 350 inhabited islands and a legendary tradition of hospitality – with such advantages the Greek tourist industry could hardly fail. Yet compared to other Mediterranean countries Greece was slow to organise its tourist potential and it was not until the late 1950s, under the encouragement of Karamanlis, that developments began. Greece had to start from scratch for the country had no tourist infrastructure; appalling roads, slow trains, old buses and ferry-boats made travel and tourism difficult, and outside Athens there were few hotels and those that existed were spartan in their amenities.

Under the auspices of the National Tourist Organisation (NTO) the Greek tourist industry now plays a major role in the economic life of the country and has built itself into an industry with foreign exchange rates amounting to one-third of the total value of Greek exports. The country experienced a considerable influx of tourists after the devaluation of the drachma in 1963 and undoubtedly a significant factor in the continued popularity of Greece as a vacation centre has been its comparatively low cost of living. But today this has altered, for currency changes in Western Europe, particularly in Britain, and rapid inflation in Greece have reduced many of the price advantages of earlier years especially to Britons, though less significantly to West Germans and Scandinavians. Its climate and tangible manifestations of earlier civilisations, however, continue to attract visitors from all over Europe (and elsewhere) and the NTO, with conservation also in mind, has wisely decided to channel future developments into specific areas. These include the islands of Crete, Corfu and the Dodecanese group (particularly Rhodes), the Argolid coast of the Peloponnesus, the Chalkidiki peninsula south-east of Thessalonica (with the exception of the Orthodox Republic of Mount Athos) and the Attica coast south-east of Athens.

At present 68 per cent of the tourist flow visits Athens for an average of three days and if this trend continues a doubling of hotel accommodation will be required; in 1976 there was a total of 25,000 tourist beds in the city. Training centres in hotel and restaurant services are becoming increasingly popular to meet the growing demands and whims of the tourist sector and the NTO is particularly anxious to encourage private activity in the tourist field, especially outside Athens where hotel complexes in provincial areas can make major economic impacts.

In order to accommodate tourism, as well as other branches of the economy, a revolution has occurred in the country's transport network. New roads and national highways have

Paraportiani Church, Myconos

been built, or are under construction, ports have been
modernised and ferry-boats and services greatly improved.
Piraeus is the centre for the inter-island boat services and an
extensive and efficient domestic air network is based on Athens.
Greece was slow to embark on railway development; the system
is restricted and topography militates against its further
extension. Many towns and archaeological sites in the
Peloponnesus, however, are served by a narrow-gauge railway
whose terminus is in Athens and the main standard railway line
from Athens to Thessalonica is connected with the European
system.

9

The Greek Way of Life

The Greek people, perhaps more than most nations and ethnic groups, are the direct product of their history which, as previous chapters have shown, has been extremely varied and invariably stormy. Standing at the crossroads where east meets west, Greece has always suffered from an identity crisis and today this is firmly embedded in the personality and national characteristics of its people. They regard themselves as European and 'western', but the traveller from the west senses in Greece the aura of the Middle East or, to use a now largely defunct term, the Levant. Coming from the east, however, even from the country's nearest geographical neighbour, Turkey, the visitor quickly becomes conscious of most of the trappings of western society. Many would argue, therefore, that the Greeks are a curious mixture of orient and occident and that the westernisation of their country is little more than a veneer. Certainly since independence they have aped western ideas and attitudes, yet their history, ancient, medieval and modern, has constantly forced them to look towards the Middle East and they share a number of characteristics and affinities with the peoples of this area.

It is in the cities and large towns that western influence is obviously most marked and both Athens and Thessalonica can boast some of the better hotels in Europe where the efficiency and service is enjoyed by Greeks and tourists alike. The now ubiquitous supermarkets, discotheques, boutiques and other western trappings also cater for the rapidly changing pattern of Greek urban life. Yet even in the centre of Athens the colours and attitudes of the orient are still strongly represented. The visitor might notice only the aromatic smell of Greek tobacco, or the souvlaki stalls with their aromas of sizzling meat and fragrant herbs, or the sound of the bouzouki and the clicking of worry beads in the hands of old men as they idly sit and gossip politics in the cafes. In reality, however, eastern attitudes go much deeper, but it is in the countryside, in spite of many economic and social changes, that the oriental face is most apparent. Here women continue to labour in the fields while their menfolk adorn the village square playing backgammon and sipping coffee. At evenings boys and girls still stroll separately and a young man cannot be seen alone with his betrothed until their marriage has been arranged and the appropriate dowry negotiated. Such negotiations, generally through a middleman, follow procedures which have changed little over the centuries and it goes without saying that chastity, or at least prudent behaviour, is highly prized among Greek girls, often forming the major, sometimes the only, part of their dowry. It is in the country, too, that the men still perform variations of their strange and soulful dances, and that elaborate local festivals under the guise of Christianity preserve many superstitious and even pagan beliefs.

NATIONAL CHARACTERISTICS

It is always difficult to characterise a nation without resorting to gross over-generalisations. It can be said, however, that the Greeks display most of the characteristics associated with the Mediterranean temperament. They are a volatile, vibrant people with a passion for noise, crowds and conversation and adjectives particularly apt in describing their general personality are generous, curious, wily, sensuous, frank and hospitable. Yet these are mere words for the Greek is a complex character and out of his crisis of identity certain national characteristics have emerged which make him unique. He has been described – by a Greek – as someone who touches the stars with one hand and the mud or dust with the other. Though a typical Greek exaggeration it is not without truth and the western philhellenes who still cling to the myth that the modern Greek is the direct descendant of the classical Greeks and the inheritor of their ideals should, perhaps, be reminded that there was a Sparta as well as an Athens whose contradictory philosophies are borne out in the modern Greek character. The Greek values friendship and is warm and generous to foreigners, but for him cunning is a virtue and one eye is firmly fixed on watching for the main chance. This is certainly not to imply that the Greek is dishonest, merely, that in his acquaintances he is anxious to meet people with influence, for patronage at all levels of society is a basic tenet. There are other aspects of the Greek character that are contradictory. He relishes new ideas, but finds it hard to sustain enthusiasm; he has a high sense of family and personal honour, but can be inhumane and even cruel; he is a brave and resilient fighter, but enjoys leisure and prefers conversation to work; he admires strength and success in others without wishing to emulate them, yet he likes to be flattered and has a strong sense of personal vanity; he spoils his children, but is not particularly tolerant to animals.

Perhaps the Greek characteristic which strikes the visitor most forcibly is that of natural curiosity and inquisitiveness – which can often reach embarrassing proportions – and this is something that has certainly not changed from ancient times. Telemachus' interrogation of Athena in the opening pages of the *Odyssey* could well be the script of a first meeting between contemporary Greek and visitor:

> Do tell me who you are and where you come from. What is your native town? Who are your people? And since you certainly cannot have come on foot, what vessel brought you here? How did the crew come to land you in Ithaca, and who did they claim to be? Then there is another thing I would like to know. Is this your first visit to Ithaca, or have my people received you before. . . .?

In a modern situation this line of attack would perhaps be more personal, involving questions on occupation, salary, age, political inclinations and family matters!

Nor is Xenios Zeus, the patron god of hospitality, dead. Greek hospitality is proverbial, but often overwhelming and vigorous, particularly on Crete, recalling Nestor's orders to his servants in regard to departing Telemachus: 'After him and force him to come back.' Throughout most of the country the goodwill to welcome the visitor and to render him a service or help is both a matter of national pride and of personal honour. Nevertheless, there are some parts of the country where visitors are treated with suspicion and avoided, and others where the mass influx of tourists has inevitably broken down the intimate contact that once existed between locals and visitors.

PHILOTIMO AND THE FAMILY

The Greek character rests on *philotimo* which roughly translated means personal honour or self-esteem rather than chauvinist pride, and it is the basis of the Greek's status within his family, village or district and, above all, of his nationalism. Individualism and improvisation, two important aspects of the Greek character, rest on *philotimo*, and it also underlies his apparent nonchalance, his tendency to take unnecessary risks and his courage, examples of which abound in history. To the democratically minded Greek, *philotimo* is something which dissolves all class barriers, for everyone, illiterate and educated, poor and wealthy is, in the Greek's view, equal to everyone else; respect is accorded the individual as a person and not because of his status or achievements. *Philotimo*, therefore, rests on inviolability and freedom. In many ways Greek behaviour is constrained by the fear of appearing ridiculous or losing face, hence drunkenness in the Anglo-Saxon sense is uncommon. As a consequence of this perhaps, the Greeks have little respect for the society drop-outs and, as far as tourists are concerned, they dislike seeing the unwashed, barefooted and shabby youth sitting on the pavements of central Athens or taking over small island towns. Yet even the penniless hitch-hikers, bound for Istanbul, Kabul and Goa, are tolerated.

Self-esteem and self-dependence in no way undermine family life. In fact the Greek family unit is very much stronger than its counterpart in Western Europe or North America and functions as a powerful and rigid social grouping. Though old ways are gradually changing, parochial ties and attitudes are very marked and family loyalties take precedence over all others. The family unit consists not merely of the husband, wife and children, but extends through a whole range of relatives to second cousins and even further. Three, even four generations often live under the same roof, for old people are automatically taken care of within the family and the opinions of grandparents and elders are respected and valued. In the same vein, children, particularly during their earlier years, are enormously indulged by their parents and other relatives and are the objects of such admiration and adoration that sometimes it amounts almost to idolatory, especially in the case of a son.

The family unit, however, is not simply a domestic association based on blood relationship but a corporate and united enterprise dedicated to the provision of its members. This may involve exploitation of its inherited fields and flocks, or work in the towns and cities, and often both. It is also a religious community protected by its icons and other personal religious objects, and the house itself is a sanctuary for its members and guests. It is this multiform character that underlies the exclusive solidarity of the Greek family, even within a tightly knit village community, and as such each member is obliged to give help to another, including financial assistance, in times of need. An old Cretan folksong seems to capture the essence and richness of the Greek family unit:

I do not envy others for their vineyards and their gardens,
I envy only those who can stay in one place.
And most I envy those who have brothers and first cousins
To grieve with them and rejoice with them
And to help each other when anything befalls.

One of the main concerns of the Greek family is the marriage and honourable establishment of the children. This is often a crucial test of the family's resources and reputation. In rural areas the Greek laws of inheritance and village custom both require that property be divided equally among all heirs, including daughters who are often entitled to their share at marriage in the form of a dowry. This system of equal inheritance is, as already indicated, at the base of many of the agricultural difficulties facing contemporary Greece. Apart from migration, one traditional solution to excessive farm fragmentation is the training or education of 'surplus' children, generally sons, for non-agricultural occupations. Sons or cousins with paper qualifications bring honour and, usually, economic benefits to the whole family unit.

Until recently arranged marriages, with great stress on the girl's dowry, were the rule and they are still common. A substantial dowry remains a traditional prerequisite in many parts of the country and marriage prospects are therefore dependent on the wealth of the relatives. In the large towns and cities dowryless marriages are becoming more common and the daughter has greater say in the choice of her marriage partner, but it is still the father who has the responsibility for conducting the matrimonial proceedings which are governed by complex points of procedure and ritual. For example, the obligation of the eldest son to see all sisters married before himself is still considered a point of honour in many families.

Of Greek weddings the country ones are naturally more picturesque and their celebrations can often continue for days. The marriage feast, accompanied by song and dance, is held in the local taverna and as at other local festivities rich peasant costumes are still worn, particularly by the older generation. Perhaps one of the most incongruous sights in rural Greece today is the spectacle of traditionally dressed parents, or at least grandparents, mingling with their jean-clad offspring.

GREEK ORTHODOXY

Greece is predominantly an Orthodox society and religion, as in the past, plays a vital role in the daily lives of its people. Ninety-five per cent of the country's population are nominally members of the Orthodox Church though, curiously, only a small percentage are regular churchgoers. Few Greeks, however, would regard themselves as non-believers and the church is virtually a symbol of Greek nationality and an essential part of Hellenism. So closely identified are church and nation that the Greek and Turkish population exchanges, discussed in Chapter 7, were carried out on a religious basis, and though not autocratic in the Roman Catholic sense, Orthodoxy is still invested with great authority and prestige and deeply involved in the political life of the country.

The doctrine of the Greek Church is largely that of the Trinitarian western churches, though differences developing over the centuries have hindered communion between east and west. During the seventeenth century Orthodoxy was strongly influenced by Calvinism and attempts towards a union were common. It is significant that today the Anglican and Orthodox Churches are in communion, whereas a wide doctrinal gulf still separates Catholicism and Orthodoxy. Provided it is left alone the Orthodox Church is singularly tolerant and proselytism is especially forbidden by the Greek Constitution. Like the Turks before them the Greeks believe that a 'disbeliever' in one religion will never be a good believer in another and one of the reasons for the traditional unpopularity of Catholicism is that throughout history it was out to propagandise. Complete religious freedom is thus recognised in Greece, but adherents to other faiths make up only small minorities; for instance, there are 35,000 Roman and Greek Catholics, 11,000 Armenian Christians, 15,000 Protestants, 8,000 Jehovah's Witnesses, 108,000 Moslems and 6,000 Jews. The latter are still found mainly in Thessalonica and the largest Roman Catholic populations, remnants of Latin influence, are chiefly in the Aegean and Ionian islands.

Although the Greek Church recognises the spiritual primacy of the Ecumenical Patriarch of Constantinople it is now a self-governing body administered by the Holy Synod under the presidency of the Archbishop of Athens and All Greece. It has no jurisdiction, however, over the church in Crete nor over the church of the Dodecanese, both of which are autonomous institutions but owe allegiance to the Ecumenical Patriarch.

The refinements of Greek Orthodox practice are complex and its liturgy involves the rites and rubrics inherited directly from Byzantium. Religion, therefore, tends to be highly formal, ritualistic and impersonal though it incorporates, especially in rural areas, much that is of local origin. To the western eye its mysticism is reminiscent of superstitious and even pagan beliefs which have been translated into occasions of religious significance. In many rural areas religious worship is a sort of 'primitive Orthodoxy' allied to folklore, and belief in the evil eye is widely prevalent. It is still common on the island of Syros, and in other parts of Greece, for a wooden cross to be nailed on the bow of a boat as a preventive against the evil eye, and the raised open hand with fingers splayed in admonishment is regarded as a curse throughout the country. So mixed is superstition with religion that even meeting a priest can often be deemed unlucky. An old tradition on Euboea was to tie a knot in a handkerchief for every priest met in the course of a day; this 'tying up the priest' was supposed to prevent the holy man from plotting mischief!

The local priest or *papas* is allowed to marry and normally he leads a similar existence to his rural or urban parishoners. His income is usually supplemented from some form of farming enterprise or by running a small business. His level of education is generally above that of his charges which earns him their confidence and his council is valued and respected. Marriage prevents the *papas* from rising in the church hierarchy and he is not allowed to preach. Instead he reads a circular sermon sent to him by the bishop. As nation and church are hard to distinguish in Greece, this circular can be as much a political treatise as an exhortation to worship and serve god. In contrast to the *papas*, Orthodox bishops and other high officials are supposedly celibate and are recruited from monastic institutions.

Monasticism plays a major role in Orthodoxy and in the past it was a vital force in preserving the Greek religious and cultural heritage during foreign rule. The number of monasteries since independence has greatly declined, though many of those surviving are rich in history, legends, architecture, frescoes and manuscripts. A unique monastic community, whose origins date from the tenth century, is the self-governing community of Mount Athos occupying the easternmost peninsula of Chalcidice. It is composed of some twenty monasteries and other religious settlements and females are barred from its territory. The Greek government recognised the autonomy of Mount Athos in the 1920s and today it is administered by a council of four members and an assembly of twenty, one deputy from each monastery. Of the monasteries, which are classified as either idiorrhythmic or cenobitic, seventeen are Greek, one Russian, one Serbian and one Bulgarian. *Sketes*, or dependent communities, are subject to one or other of the ruling monasteries and hermits and monks who follow a semi-eremitical form of life are also a feature of Mount Athos.

Another unique monastic community is that at Meteora, near Kalabaka, in Thessaly where a series of monasteries lies perched at great heights on precipitous rock pinnacles. They were originally founded in the fourteenth century when, as in Athos, monks fleeing from brigandage took refuge in inaccessible retreats which served as hermitages. As their numbers increased the basis of a monastic community was established. The Meteora monasteries were formerly reached either by precarious jointed ladders which the monks drew up in times of danger, or by a net or box attached to a long rope and hoisted up with the aid of a pulley. Visiting them today, although still arduous, is much simplified by a series of stairways and ramps cut into the rock faces. Like the Athos monasteries, those of Meteora are also rich in frescoes, icons and other works of religious art.

Numerous other monasteries are found throughout Greece, though the term *monastiri* is also applied to lonely chapels and recalls the former use of these places by hermits.

CHURCH STYLE AND DECORATION

The Greek landscape is dominated by the material manifestations of Orthodoxy. All villages and every district or suburb in towns and cities have at least one domed, Byzantine-style church which forms the centre of the local community and in rural areas is closely associated with the village school. The church, dedicated to the saint of the district, is the pride of the local inhabitants and its lavish decoration and pretentiousness contrast with the humbler buildings of rural communities.

Churches and wayside shrines also appear as isolated features of the landscape, particularly on hill-tops or on coastal promontories. Many are small and are used only on one day of the year to commemorate a particular saint or the name-day of the founder.

The traditional form of the Orthodox church, current throughout Greece, is the cross-in-square structure surmounted by a central dome. Symbolically the dome and the cross mark the union of heaven and earth, or the two natures of the incarnate Christ. The impression of architectural simplicity is deceptive however. Numerous Greek churches, often with ornate detail, date back to Byzantine foundations, but even new churches slavishly follow the traditional architectural form. In those areas where Latin rule remained longest church styles were modified. On Corfu, and the Ionian islands generally, is a style which has been termed 'Ionian-Baroque' and dates from the seventeenth and eighteenth centuries. It is exemplified in St Spiridion's Church in Corfu town and in the Platytera monastery on its outskirts; one of the distinguishing features of the style is a free-standing campanile topped with a painted dome. Byzantine-style belfrys, especially on the Ionian islands, usually consisted of an ornamental wall pierced with arches for bells. They stood either above the façade of the church or over its courtyard gate.

The interior design of most Greek churches follows a traditional and symbolic pattern. The main body of the church, the nave, is separated from the altar or sanctuary by a tall screen (the *iconostasis*) beyond which only the priest is normally allowed to enter. This separation of priest from congregation symbolises the division between the divine and the human, or between the spiritual and material worlds. Yet at the same time it unites the two for the screen, often of beautifully carved wood, is adorned with icons which portray this double function, representing the world that stands midway between the sensible and the spiritual. Icons are also placed on stands and on walls, and often the whole interior wall-surface of the church is decorated with frescoes. The veneration of holy images is a central aspect of the Orthodox ritual for the images are

Byzantine Church, Skopelos

regarded as testimonies of the process of transfiguration and in them is felt to be present something of the deified reality of the prototypes – Christ, the Virgin, saints and angels. Many are covered with small silver votives, the intention being to put a prayer or petition into visible form. These may be small images of a sailor or soldier for whose safety the parents or family is concerned. A limb, a hand, a heart or a body represents prayers for recovery of health. Eventually these simulcra are melted down to add more silver (and often gold) adornment to their respective icons.

Thus in architecture and in decoration the Greek church is a visible projection of the spiritual world. The Greeks are firm believers in divine-human co-operation and in divine intervention. All faculties, physical and mental, are used in worship – hence the need for holy relics, incense, candles, colours and chanting.

The Saints

From what has already been said it is clear that the saints play a very important part in Greek life and their functions and names often prove that they are the descendants of the old Greek deities, the new religion having been grafted on to the old. Every steamer has its icon of St Nicholas in the cabin, before which a tiny lamp is kept burning and a church or monastery of that patron saint of sailors often stands on or near the site of a temple of Poseidon. Helios, the sun-god, has been succeeded by Prophet Elias, whose chapels crown almost every eminence in Greece; the Virgin has replaced Athena, and the Parthenon in the Middle Ages was the Church of St Mary, whether as a Greek cathedral or as a Latin bishop's seat; St Dionysios has dethroned Dionysios; the story of St George and the Dragon is the Christian version of Theseus and the minotaur, so that the Theseion temple in Athens naturally became the Church of St George.

Each place in Greece has its local saint: Corfu boasts of St Spiridion (after whom numerous Corfiotes are named), Cefalonia of St Gerasimos, Patras of St Andrew, Zakinthos of St Dionysios and Thessalonica of St Demetrios. Each district celebrates its patron saint in a festival, and scarcely a day passes without one of these celebrations. Perhaps the most striking religious processions are those in honour of Corfu's St Spiridion, when four times a year his mummified body is borne through the town with full military honours. This commemorates the times when he delivered the island from the Turks, pestilence and famine; his miraculous powers are also directed to less spectacular events – a policeman cured of epilepsy, for example, or the evil eye averted, or an old man cured of foul language. There is further evidence of his dealings against croup, diphtheria and lice.

As with the names of the saints, many of the feasts and festivals connected with them can be traced back in history, often to ancient times. Even the Easter celebrations, for example, the most spectacular festival in the Orthodox calender, probably stems from the Lesser Eleusinia – the return of Persephone and the general awakening of nature after the winter months. The most important festival for the individual is his or her name-day, which for the Greek takes the place of the birthday – an arrangement particularly favoured by Athenian matrons since it obscures the actual age of the celebrant! Most Greeks are named after a saint, but those called after past heroes and notables celebrate their name-day on All Saints Day. One should not be surprised to find names such as Xenophon, Alcibiades, Demosthenes, Penelope, Antigone, Adonis and Olympia applied to ordinary citizens.

THE GREEK LANGUAGE

Language has been the other major pillar in the cultural cohesion of the Greeks though internally it has often had a disuniting influence. Modern Greek, which is spoken by 95 per cent of the country's population, is a natural development from classical Greek, through *koine* or New Testament Greek, and Byzantine or medieval Greek, to the present day. Like all languages it has undergone various changes in pronunciation, grammar and vocabulary throughout its historical course, but the modern tongue has preserved a remarkable number of qualities of the original stock and has maintained a unity unparalleled by any other European language. It is often pointed out that the oldest literature in the Greek language, the Homeric epic poems, is far more intelligible to the modern Greek than Chaucer is to English speakers.

The fact remains, however, that modern Greek is a language in transition and one that is experimental in form and open to new usages and influences. A striking feature of the modern language is the instability of spelling found even among the commonest words. Many of these differences arise from the distinction between the 'demotic' and 'puristic' forms of speech. Colloquial Greek is a mixture of both, with demotic predominating. The puristic form, *katharevousa* (whose origins were discussed in Chapter 6), is much more formal in style and used mainly in writing official documents, some textbooks and partly in newspapers, the latter employing a mixed speech known as *kathomiloumeni*.

The language issue, like so many issues in Greece, is a political one and the fierce struggle between the adherents of the extreme forms has often incited riots and even overthrown governments. According to Francis King (*Introducing Greece*) 'those writers who are most fervid in their support of the extreme form of demotic are usually of the left, and are not infrequently accused by their opponents of being communists; whereas those university professors whose textbooks are produced in an academic Greek so refined as to be all but unintelligible to their students are of the right.' Though the distinction may not be quite as clear cut, there is, nonetheless, important evidence of the political significance of the language question. The so-called Gospel Riots of November 1901, for example, largely arose out of the indignation of students and others at the translation of the New Testament into the vernacular. It led to the overthrow of the government at this time. In November 1903 Athens was further convulsed by riots because Aeschylus' *Oresteia* had been adapted and presented at the theatre in a modern Greek version which was considered to contain certain vulgar expressions. The conflict has continued and the gulf which now exists is well illustrated in the press where political news is printed in the official language and the serialised stories and the more popular items in the demotic tongue.

The language question has certainly complicated the Greek education system, perhaps more than any other single factor, for the question as to whether the demotic or *katharevousa* tongue should be the medium of teaching has virtually meant that with every change of government there has been a change in the medium of education. From the liberalisation policies of Papandreou, the military government reverted to the system of teaching children above third grade in elementary school in *katharevousa* Greek. The current system under Karamanlis is now considerably modified, but it is not difficult to understand why Greek education this century has borne the imprint of confusion.

Visitors to Greece are strongly advised to be familiar at least with the Greek alphabet. This is indispensable for reading street and bus signs and once mastered the number of Greek words that have their direct equivalent in English will be appreciated. No one can pretend that modern Greek is an easy language, but any attempt to speak it is warmly appreciated by the Greeks. In country districts a few Greek words and phrases can lead to invitations for coffee or ouzo, fishing trips and sometimes overnight accommodation in a villager's home.

NOTHING IN EXCESS

Dionysos, a son of Zeus and a Theban princess, was the ancient god of the grape and thus of drinking. His disorderly escapades in the wild company of Satyrs and Maenads are illustrated in various forms of Greek art and the Dionysian myths make constant reference to the devastating effects of strong wine. Whether the contemporary Greeks have taken these warnings to heart is debatable. Drunkenness, as already implied, is certainly not a common sight, but the oft-quoted assertion that the Greeks are moderate drinkers is regarded by Kenneth Young (*The Greek Passion*) as 'a myth floated by Methodists on tour'. The Greek glass, he emphasises, is really an ordinary tumbler and although etiquette demands that it must be never more than a third full, it is constantly replenished. The numerous religious festivals, anniversaries, birthdays and national holidays (not to mention the wine festivals held during the summer as part of the country's tourist programme) are all marked by the liberal consumption of wine and slight inebriation is considered a necessary part of enjoyment. The claim that most Greeks are sober citizens is also coloured by their passion for other liquids, coffee in particular, but also soft drinks and water. The later is considered one of the greatest delicacies and Greeks who claim to distinguish between different qualities of water according to the spring from which it was drawn are not boasting. The water jug is an integral part of every meal and a glass is served as an accompaniment to coffee, ice-cream and sweetmeats.

Vines, along with olives and grains, are a traditional mainstay of Mediterranean agriculture and ancient Greek literature makes constant reference to the place of wines in Greek life. An ancient practice was the addition of resin as a means of strengthening the poorer quality wines which were sourish and difficult to keep. In the twelfth century the Metropolitan of Athens, wishing to give a friend some idea of the flavour of resin, wrote to him that it 'seems to be pressed from the juice of the pine rather than from that of the grape'. This practice unique to Greece, has survived the centuries and is represented today by *retsina* which, though an acquired taste, is an excellent foil to the oily character of Greek food. The country, however, produces a large variety of unresinated wines and there are many regional specialities.

Whereas retsina and other wines are popular throughout Greece, the middle-class fashion favours the more expensive lager beer which is considered an elegant drink. *Hellas Fix* is the Greek rendering of Fuchs, a Bavarian brewer who accompanied King Otho to his kingdom and by his industry assured the Athenian and Greek public a constant supply of excellent lager. *Alpha, Amstel* and other brands also stand up well to better known European brands.

Ouzo is the spirit of the country and is a deceptively strong drink. It is related both to raki and to the sweeter mastika and is distilled from the lees of the wine pips and skins with added anise to give it flavour. The Greeks drink ouzo as an aperitif or at any time they think fit and it is usually taken with what the Greeks call *mezé* – appetisers or hors d'oeuvres.

GREECE A LA CARTE

Greece and Britain have one basic characteristic in common – in neither country would a gourmet travel for the sake of the food. Tourist brochures which describe Greek cooking as 'combining the delicacies of French cuisine with the succulence of the East' and Athens as a 'gourmet's paradise' are misleading to say the least. As one writer recently put it 'Greek food is never good enough to travel for and never bad enough to keep anyone away'. The average Greek enjoys eating out, but this is purely a social function for he is not a fastidious gastronome and modern Greek culinary talents as revealed in the majority of restaurants and tavernas are extremely limited. The prodigious use of olive oil is not generally appreciated by the western palate, but this, along with spices and herbs is one of the basic ingredients in Greek cuisine.

The taverna is the typical Greek eating place but the distinction between it and a restaurant proper is nowadays not easily definable for there are 'de luxe' tavernas which are more sophisticated and expensive than the lower quality restaurants. Generally, the menu of the restaurant offers a range of dishes, while the fare in the taverna is uncompromisingly Greek and often limited to a few specialities prepared by the owner himself. The atmosphere is informal and friendly, but the service is erratic and often slapdash. For the Greek who visits a taverna, however, food is not the first objective. He goes to enjoy an evening out with his family and friends, to sit, converse and to hear popular music. Many of the 'fashionable' tavernas of the Athenian Plaka district put on elaborate floor shows to attract tourists, but much more authentic, and certainly more down-to-earth, are the dock-side establishments in Piraeus.

The Zakharoplasteion
Zakharoplasteion is one of the numerous lengthy Greek signs on which visitors like to test their mastery, or otherwise, of Greek pronunciation. In certain instances the word is made all the more formidable by the addition of the prefix Galakto-, which results in a word of twenty-three letters, one fewer than the total number contained in the modern Greek alphabet. 'Café' appears a diminutive and insignificant translation for such a term, but essentially that is what the zakharoplasteion is, an establishment selling a wide range of drinks, ice-creams, cakes and confections. It is extremely popular with the Greeks, who have a very sweet tooth, and the zakharoplasteia proliferate all over the capital, its suburbs and the main squares of all towns. They are patronised until well after midnight in summer (some in the Kolonaki district of Athens are open all night) and they serve as important social venues. All Greek towns have certain establishments where socialites gather to see and be

seen. In Corfu it is the Liston, the arcade of pavement cafés at the northern end of the Esplanade, whereas in Rhodes the town's social centre is among the cafés and restaurants of Mandraki Harbour. Athens has numerous such centres though Constitution Square, in spite of its inflated prices, remains the most popular among Athenians and tourists alike.

During the summer months a visit to a zakharoplasteion is always preceded by the evening *peripato* or *volta*. This is particularly popular on Sundays when the whole population of a town seems to be strolling along the main streets, parading themselves as much as enjoying the night air.

The Kafeneion

The Greeks are apt to take slight offence at the association of their national beverage with the name of their age-old and far from dormant enemy. Yet their coffee is definitely Turkish and the name sounds more exotic than Greek, and infinitely more oriental than Nescafé. Turkish coffee comes in tiny cups and in various gradations of sweetness. As the sugar is added during its preparation the Greeks specify their requirements by ordering either *gliko* (very sweet), or *metrio* (medium) or *pikro* (bitter), though these are only some of the gradations. Inevitably it is accompanied by a glass of water, which for the uninitiated is useful for washing down the muddy lees unsuspectingly supped up from the bottom of the cup.

The *kafeneion* is the traditional home of Turkish coffee and its dedicated clientele, still exclusively male, convince the visitor that coffee drinking is another Greek national pastime. This, however, is a mistake, as much business is transacted in the coffee house, appointments are made and kept, and the latest news, political and commercial, is exchanged and discussed. In rural Greece the coffee house is the key social institution in the village where inhabitants meet to discuss agricultural problems and community affairs. Whether in town or in village the coffee house is where public opinion is formed, and it is here that local and national politicians must win their battles. Indeed, during elections, the coffee houses are the arenas where candidates for political office deliver their speeches and vie for votes.

ORGANISED ENTERTAINMENT

In Greece organised entertainment tends to be confined to the cities and larger towns, though even modest provincial centres and small island capitals have their ever-popular cinemas. In summer these are open-air and the cinema has been able to combat the appeal of television, at least for part of the year.

Athens is the centre of the country's cultural life and has numerous theatres, including the National Theatre which was founded in 1900. The city is also the home of the National Opera Company of Greece and the Athens State Orchestra which by favouring the works of modern Greek composers has done much to lay the foundations of Greece's musical life. However Greek popular music has made a greater impact abroad than its serious music. Much must be attributed to the successful 1960 film *Never on Sunday*, which showed that the Greeks had something new and fresh to offer the popular music world. Its score was by Manos Hadjidakis, a serious composer who, like Mikis Theodorakis, has turned his creative ability to the infinitely more profitable film and popular markets.

The music of Hadjidakis, Theodorakis, Xarhakos and many others is essentially folksong and folk-dance music with overtones of popular music from abroad. It incorporates a variety of subtle influences, many of them stemming from the east and echoing the past and the tragic history of the country. The music is tied mainly to love themes (tender, passionate, jealous) and also to grief, death and religion, and emphasises the peasant background of the country and the strong melancholic, even fatalistic, streak in the Greek character. Yet it is extremely colourful and vigorous; its dynamic sound comes from the bouzouki, an instrument brought to Greece by the refugees from Asia Minor in the 1920s. A decade ago the cult of the bouzouki was particularly strong in Greece and it still remains a characteristic sound in the Athenian Plaka and in the tavernas and restaurants of the Saronic coast. Male solo and formation dancing form an integral part of the atmosphere of the bouzoukia. The ban by the former government on the smashing of wine glasses when fervour is high has now been lifted!

Bibliography

Admiralty, Naval Intelligence Division, *Greece* (*3 volumes London, 1943*)

Andrews, K., *Athens* (Dent, 1967)

Boardman, J., *The Greeks Overseas* (Penguin Books, 1964)

Bowman, J., *The Travellers' Guide to Crete* (Jonathan Cape, 1972)

Bradford, E., *The Companion Guide to the Greek Islands* (Collins, 1970)

Brockway, L. and G., *Greece: A Classical Tour with Extras* (Victor Gollancz, 1967)

Clogg, R. (ed), *The Struggle for Greek Independence* (Macmillan, 1973)

—— and Yannopoulos, G. (eds), *Greece under Military Rule* (Secker & Warburg, 1972)

Clutton, E. and Kenny, A., *Crete* (David & Charles, 1977)

Cottrell, L., *The Bull of Minos* (Pan Books, 1955)

Currie, J., *The Travellers' Guide to Rhodes and the Dodecanese* (Jonathan Cape, 1970)

Darby, H. C. (ed), *A Short History of Greece* (Cambridge University Press, 1965)

Dicks, B., *Corfu* (David & Charles, 1977)

—— *Rhodes* (David & Charles, 1974)

—— *The Greeks: How They Live and Work* (David & Charles, 1971)

Durrell, L., *Prospero's Cell* (Faber & Faber, 1970)

—— *Reflections on a Marine Venus* (Faber & Faber, 1969)

Eliot, A., *Greece* (Time-Life, 1964)

Finley, M. I., *The World of Odysseus* (Penguin Books, 1967)

Fodor, E., *Greece* (Fodor's Modern Guides, 1960)

Hearsey, J. E. N., *City of Constantine 324–1453* (John Murray, 1963)

Herodotus, *History of the Greek and Persian War* (New English Library, 1966)

Homer, *The Iliad* trans Rieu, E. V. (Penguin Books, 1961)

—— *The Odyssey* trans Rieu, E. V. (Penguin Books, 1964)

Howarth, D., *The Greek Adventure* (Collins, 1976)

Hutchinson, R. W., *Prehistoric Crete* (Penguin Books, 1962)

Jongh, Brian de, *The Companion Guide to Southern Greece* (Collins, 1971)

King, F. (ed), *Introducing Greece* (Methuén, 1956)

Kitto, H. D. F., *The Greeks* (Penguin Books, 1951)

Lancaster, O., *Classical Landscape with Figures* (John Murray, 1975)

Luce, J. V., *The End of Atlantis* (Thames & Hudson, 1969)

Miller, W., *Essays on the Latin Orient* (Cambridge University Press, 1921)

—— *The Latins in the Levant – a History of Frankish Greece 1204–1566* (Cambridge University Press, 1906; reprinted 1964)

—— *The Ottoman Empire and its Successors 1801–1827* (Cambridge University Press, 1936)

Mylonas, G. E., *Mycenae, A Guide to its Ruins and its History* (Athens, 1973)

Nagel Travel Guide, *Greece* (Nagel, Geneva, 1965)

Payne, R., *The Splendour of Greece* (Robert Hale, 1961)

Rice, D. T., *The Byzantines* (Thames & Hudson, 1962)

Rossiter, S. (ed), *The Blue Guide to Greece* (Benn, 1967)

St. Clair, W., *That Greece Might Be Free: The Philhellenes in the War of Independence* (Oxford University Press, 1972)

Sicilianos, D., *Old And New Athens* trans Liddell, R. (Putnam, 1960)

Smith, M. L., *Ionian Vision: Greece in Asia Minor 1919–1922* (Allen Lane, 1973)

Thucydides, *History of the Peloponnesian War* trans Warner, R., (Penguin Books, 1966)

Whitting, P. (ed), *Byzantium: An Introduction* (Blackwell, 1971)

Woodhouse, C. M., *Modern Greece, A Short History* (Faber & Faber, 1968)

Wunderlich, H. G., *The Secret of Crete* (Fontana/Collins, 1976)

Young, K., *The Greek Passion* (Dent, 1969)

Zakythinos, D. A., *The Making of Modern Greece* trans Johnstone, K. R. (Blackwell, 1976)

Index